Economic Policy Reforms 2018

GOING FOR GROWTH INTERIM REPORT

This work is published under the responsibility of the Secretary-General of the OECD. The opinions expressed and arguments employed herein do not necessarily reflect the official views of OECD member countries.

This document, as well as any data and any map included herein, are without prejudice to the status of or sovereignty over any territory, to the delimitation of international frontiers and boundaries and to the name of any territory, city or area.

Please cite this publication as:
OECD (2018), *Economic Policy Reforms 2018: Going for Growth Interim Report*, OECD Publishing, Paris.
http://dx.doi.org/10.1787/growth-2018-en

ISBN 978-92-64-29195-9 (print)
ISBN 978-92-64-29197-3 (PDF)

Series: Economic Policy Reforms
ISSN 1813-2715 (print)
ISSN 1813-2723 (online)

The statistical data for Israel are supplied by and under the responsibility of the relevant Israeli authorities. The use of such data by the OECD is without prejudice to the status of the Golan Heights, East Jerusalem and Israeli settlements in the West Bank under the terms of international law.

Photo credits: Cover © Alain Jacoby-Koaly pour Studio Pykha.

Corrigenda to OECD publications may be found on line at: *www.oecd.org/about/publishing/corrigenda.htm*.

Going for Growth *was launched in 2005 as a new form of structural surveillance complementing the OECD's long-standing country and sector-specific surveys. In line with the OECD's 1960 founding Convention, the aim is to help promote vigorous sustainable economic growth and improve the well-being of OECD citizens.*

This surveillance is based on a systematic and in-depth analysis of structural policies and their outcomes across OECD members, relying on a set of internationally comparable and regularly updated policy indicators with a well-established link to performance. Using these indicators, alongside the expertise of OECD committees and staff, policy priorities and recommendations are derived for each member and, progressively since the 2011 issue, several non-member countries (Argentina, Brazil, the People's Republic of China, Colombia, Costa Rica, India, Indonesia, Lithuania, the Russian Federation and South Africa). From one issue to the next, Going for Growth follows up on how these recommendations and priorities evolve, not least as a result of governments taking action on the identified policy priorities.

Underpinning this type of benchmarking is the observation that drawing lessons from mutual success and failure is a powerful avenue for progress. While allowance should be made for genuine differences in social preferences across OECD members, the uniqueness of national circumstances should not serve to justify inefficient policies.

In gauging performance, the focus has traditionally been on average income, productivity and employment. In order to better reflect the multi-dimensional nature of well-being the Going for Growth *framework for selecting priorities now considers inclusiveness as a prime objective, alongside productivity and employment. For this purpose, inclusiveness encompasses dimensions such as inequality and poverty, job quantity and job quality, along with labour market inclusion of vulnerable groups, gender gaps and equity in education, and health outcomes.*

In the aim of ensuring that Going for Growth *objectives are fulfilled in a way that is sustainable and improves broader well-being, policy reform priorities and recommendations need to take into account environmental pressures and risks. Hence, the* Going for Growth *framework is now also gradually integrating environmental considerations.*

Going for Growth *is the fruit of a joint effort across a large number of OECD Departments.*

http://www.oecd.org/eco/growth/going-for-growth

Editorial: An opportunity that governments should not miss

Global growth is finally back to cruising speed. For the first time in many years, all the major regions of the world are enjoying a widespread and largely synchronised upswing, even if some economies have been in steady expansion for much longer than others. Hopefully, the stagnation of living standards endured by a large share of the population in many OECD economies is coming to an end. The more rapid decline in unemployment seen in recent months is clearly an encouraging sign. However, the improvements in labour markets have yet to translate into significant and broad-based wage gains. Comprehensive structural reforms are needed to sustain stronger growth beyond the cyclical upswing, create more and better paying jobs, improve opportunities and strengthen inclusion.

Based on the review of actions taken on structural policy priorities presented in this *Going for Growth* report, there is little sign of an imminent pick-up in the pace of reforms. If anything, the review points to a further slowdown in 2017 from the already modest pace observed in the previous two years. Notwithstanding, some countries have managed to introduce significant reforms in the past year. In Japan, measures have been taken to improve access to childcare services, helping women to stay in the labour force. France has implemented a broad labour market reform, covering both employment protection legislation and collective wage bargaining. India has rolled out a goods and services tax, while Argentina has just passed a comprehensive tax reform.

By and large, governments have continued to devote greater attention to employment and social protection, including also through measures to improve healthcare services. Examples include Greece and Italy, where significant measures have been taken to strengthen social protection, as well as China, where access to healthcare for migrant workers has been improved. The broader attention to employment and income support is important for achieving greater inclusiveness and a more balanced distribution of income. To a large extent, reform efforts are paying off: the employment rates of low-skilled and youth – still low in some countries hardest hit by the crisis – are improving and already roughly back to their pre-crisis levels on average across countries, while the labour-force participation of women continues to rise.

However, significant reforms have remained too few and far between to boost productivity and to reduce the reliance on macro-policy stimulus. The return of higher global growth offers a window of opportunity to make renewed progress on structural reforms, with higher chances that they bear fruit more rapidly. Individually and collectively, decision makers need to find ways to overcome political resistance to reforms that address well-known growth bottlenecks, and lay the groundwork for their economies to make the most of the ongoing digital transformation. Higher and more sustained growth would also help to reduce financial risks related to the high public and private debt levels built up in a low interest rate environment.

While finally gathering momentum, business investment still remains weak in comparison with past expansions. Furthermore, recent data shows that investment in digital technologies, which is fundamental to boosting productivity, varies greatly across countries and firms. The growing productivity gap between leading and lagging firms is itself a source of growing wage inequality and productivity slowdown. OECD analysis suggests that firms face various constraints affecting both their incentives and capabilities to invest in such technologies.

Raising investment incentives requires measures to create a more competitive business environment, notably by promoting the entry of firms through lower regulatory barriers to start-ups and by reducing obstacles to foreign direct investment. Despite progress in these areas – for example in the European Union with the recent Services Package -- entry in business services in countries such as France, Germany and Spain is still hampered by administrative and regulatory barriers. Meanwhile, more needs to been done to reduce barriers to foreign investment where they remain relatively high, including Indonesia, Mexico and Russia. And, trade protectionism can only harm investment by raising costs and uncertainty, eroding the competitive environment and narrowing the scope for successful firms to grow.

There is also scope in many countries for reforming insolvency regimes to facilitate the orderly exit or restructuring of unsuccessful firms. This is important both to encourage experimentation of new ideas and to free the resources needed for successful innovative firms to expand. Chapter 3 of this Report presents new OECD indicators of insolvency regimes across countries, laying out the main design features to achieve such objectives. In countries such as Australia, Italy and South Africa, lowering barriers to corporate restructuring in case of distress is a priority. Reforms are also needed to harmonise insolvency procedures across member states in the European Union.

Taxation is another area where governments can act to raise private incentives to invest. This includes reforms of tax systems to broaden the tax base through the elimination of loopholes, not least those that mostly benefit individuals with high levels of income or wealth, while making room for rate reductions, especially on more mobile sources such as capital and labour income. Reforms along those lines have been implemented in countries such as Argentina, Canada and Spain, while corporate tax rates have been reduced in the United States. But reforms have yet to tackle a key distortion of tax systems, which is to favour debt over equity financing. Not only does such a bias contribute to making growth overly dependent on debt, but it also discriminates against innovative young firms.

More broadly, most countries have ample scope for reforms that can reconcile growth and inclusiveness objectives, notably by relying more on tax revenues from immovable property and inheritance. Internationally, in the effort to make corporate taxation fairer and more transparent, progress is being made to limit tax avoidance by multinationals through the so-called Base Erosion and Profit Shifting (BEPS) action plan elaborated under the auspices of the G20 and the OECD and the rolling out of the automatic exchange of information.

In countries such as India, Indonesia and Turkey, but also Italy and Greece, labour informality remains a key challenge for boosting inclusive growth. Addressing this requires reforms of burdensome product and labour regulations, along with reducing labour tax wedges on low-paid workers where they remain high. Bringing more workers in formal jobs will offer better prospects to improve skills and productivity while providing them with better social protection. In China, further measures to provide more equal access to public services while abolishing the household registration system, would promote labour mobility, productivity and inclusion. The effectiveness of reforms in these areas is best supported by the successful implementation of measures to reinforce the fight against corruption - such as the steps taken in Mexico - and to strengthen the rule of law.

In both emerging and advanced economies, the shortage of skills, including managerial and organisational talent, is one factor limiting the capabilities of many firms to adopt digital technologies. A longer-term response is reforms of education and training systems to ensure that workers acquire the cognitive and non-cognitive skills that the new digital technologies and knowledge-based capital make increasingly necessary. This includes measures to facilitate access to education for disadvantaged groups so as to reduce the digital divide. In the shorter term, the response to the skills shortage consists in providing workers with better opportunities for up-skilling and reducing the mismatch between the skills provided by workers and those demanded by employers. Developing training and life-long learning programmes that benefit those who need them most remains a challenge shared by most countries.

Hence, in spite of stronger economic growth this is no time for complacency. *Going for Growth* provides policy priorities and recommendations to unlock skills development and innovation capacity, to promote business dynamism and the diffusion of knowledge, and to help workers benefit from a fast-changing labour market. In the spirit of ensuring the sustainability of the gains in incomes and wellbeing it also increasingly takes into account environmental risks and bottlenecks (see Chapter 2). The current economic upswing provides a window for the successful implementation of reforms that can best achieve the objective of strong, inclusive and sustainable growth. The opportunity should not be missed.

Álvaro Pereira
OECD Acting Chief Economist

Table of contents

ISO Codes

The codes for country names and currencies used in this volume are those attributed to them by the International Organization for Standardization (ISO).

Country code	Country name	Currency code
ARG	Argentina	ARS
AUS	Australia	AUD
AUT	Austria	EUR
BEL	Belgium	EUR
BRA	Brazil	BRL
CAN	Canada	CAD
CHE	Switzerland	CHF
CHL	Chile	CLP
CHN	China	CNY
COL	Colombia	COP
CRI	Costa Rica	CRC
CZE	Czech Republic	CZK
DEU	Germany	EUR
DNK	Denmark	DKK
ESP	Spain	EUR
EST	Estonia	EUR
FIN	Finland	EUR
FRA	France	EUR
GBR	United Kingdom	GBP
GRC	Greece	EUR
HUN	Hungary	HUF
IDN	Indonesia	IDR
IND	India	INR
IRL	Ireland	EUR
ISL	Iceland	ISK
ISR	Israel	ILS
ITA	Italy	EUR
JPN	Japan	JPY
KOR	Republic of Korea	KRW
LTU	Lithuania	EUR
LUX	Luxembourg	EUR
LVA	Latvia	LVL
MEX	Mexico	MXN
NLD	Netherlands	EUR
NOR	Norway	NOK
NZL	New Zealand	NZD
POL	Poland	PLN
PRT	Portugal	EUR
RUS	Russian Federation	RUB
SVK	Slovak Republic	SKK
SVN	Slovenia	EUR
SWE	Sweden	SEK
TUR	Turkey	TRL
USA	United States	USD
ZAF	South Africa	ZAR

Note: EU refers to the average of 22 European Union members of the OECD.

Executive Summary

At nearly 4 per cent projected for 2018, the annual GDP growth rate of the global economy is close to the pace of growth preceding the great recession. This period of strong and broadly-based global growth creates favourable conditions for the successful implementation of structural reforms – necessary to turn the upswing into stronger and sustainable long-term growth for all.

Amid these positive short-term developments, still underpinned by supportive fiscal and monetary policy, medium and longer-term challenges remain for policy makers. Productivity growth is still disappointing. Despite the long-awaited employment recovery, wages have so far failed to follow, and many vulnerable groups are still confronted with weak prospects in the labour market. Inequality is persistent and on a longer-term trend rise within many countries – indicating that parts of society have not benefited much from growth. On top of this, megatrends such as digitalisation, environmental pressures and demographics, may carry risks for the sustainability of long-term growth unless the policy challenges they raise are properly addressed.

Going for Growth provides policy makers with concrete reform recommendations in areas which are identified as the top five country-specific priorities in order to tackle medium-term challenges, revive productivity and employment growth, while ensuring a broad sharing of the benefits. The priorities are identified building on OECD expertise on structural policy reforms and inclusive growth. The areas covered are diverse, including product and labour market regulation, education and training, tax and transfer systems, as well as trade and investment rules, physical and legal infrastructure and innovation policies. Policy recommendations across these areas are articulated so as to form a coherent reform strategy, which is crucial to reap synergies, manage trade-offs and ensure that the benefits are broadly shared over time. As such, the *Going for Growth* framework has been instrumental in helping G20 countries make progress on their structural reform agenda, including through monitoring their growth strategies to achieve sustained and balanced growth.

This *Interim* report reviews progress on structural reforms with respect to priorities identified in *Going for Growth* 2017.

Actions taken on policy priorities

- In 2017, the pace of reforms has remained similar to the relatively slow pace observed in the last two years and below the one observed in the direct aftermath of the crisis.
- Nevertheless, some bold actions have been taken – over one third of actions implemented in 2017 can be viewed as "major steps". Notable examples include reforms to strengthen social protection in Greece and Italy, a long-overdue reform of the labour market in France, significant measures in Japan to increase childcare

capacity, a goods and services tax in India and a comprehensive tax reform in Argentina, to be phased in over the next 5 years.

- More generally, the intensity of reforms has varied across policy areas. Among reforms to *boost skills acquisition and innovative capacity*, widespread actions were taken to increase the size and efficiency of R&D support.
- The bulk of actions taken to *promote business dynamism and knowledge diffusion* have focused on strengthening physical and legal infrastructure as well as on making product market regulation more competition-friendly.
- Significant actions have been taken in the area of social benefits, which is important for social cohesion. To further *help workers to cope with potentially rapid changes in jobs and tasks*, more reforms are needed in complementary areas, such as improving active labour market and housing market policies to facilitate the job-market transition and mobility.

Special chapters – reviewing indicators to enrich the *Going for Growth* analysis

This report includes two special chapters that review indicators for extending the scope of the *Going for Growth* framework: green growth indicators and OECD indicators of insolvency regimes.

The links between green and growth: what the indicators reveal

The ability to sustain long-term improvements in GDP and well-being, as advocated in *Going for Growth,* depends – among other things - on the ability to reduce negative effects (such as pollution) associated with economic activity, minimise environment-related risks and lower the reliance on (limited) natural capital resources. Hence, a more systematic approach to environment-related challenges in *Going for Growth* is warranted. At the same time, the links between the environment, environmental policies and economic growth are complex. In that regard, Chapter 2 reviews the indicators available and the recent progress made on the measurement of environmental outcomes and policies. While no single broadly-accepted measure of environmental performance exists, significant progress has been made in the measurement of green growth, notably as part of the OECD Green Growth Indicators, paving the way for a more consistent treatment of green growth in *Going for Growth.*

Facilitating orderly exit: insights from the new OECD insolvency regimes indicators

Poorly performing insolvency regimes can be linked to three inter-related sources of labour productivity weakness: the survival of so-called "zombie" firms – that should otherwise exit the market; capital miss-allocation, i.e. the trapping of resources in low productivity uses; and stalling technological diffusion. Chapter 3 presents the newly developed OECD indicators of insolvency regimes, which will allow the extension and fine-tuning of reform recommendations on exit policies in *Going for Growth.* The analysis reveals significant cross-country differences in the extent to which insolvency regimes promote orderly exit of non-viable firms, indicating that some countries have scope to improve resource allocation and productivity through reforms of bankruptcy laws and procedures.

Chapter 1. Overview of structural reforms actions in 2017

This chapter reviews the main growth challenges faced by advanced and emerging economies and takes stock of the progress made in 2017 in the adoption and implementation of structural policy reforms to address these challenges. Progress is assessed on the basis of actions taken in response to Going for Growth *policy recommendations formulated in the previous edition.*

The statistical data for Israel are supplied by and under the responsibility of the relevant Israeli authorities. The use of such data by the OECD is without prejudice to the status of the Golan Heights, East Jerusalem and Israeli settlements in the West Bank under the terms of international law.

Main Findings

- A robust and widespread pick-up in activity creates favourable conditions for the successful implementation of structural reforms, which are necessary for the current upswing to be turned into stronger and sustainable long-term growth for all.
- Yet, this opportunity risks being wasted. In 2017, the pace of reforms has, on average across countries, remained similar to the relatively slow pace observed in the last two years. In both advanced and emerging economies, there are little signs of a return to the higher pace observed a few years back.
    - In 2017, policy actions across advanced economies have been implemented in just over one tenth of the 2017 *Going for Growth* priority areas, while reforms are underway in about one third of them.
    - In emerging-market economies, even fewer concrete actions have been fully implemented. Further reforms are in the process of implementation, covering one quarter of Going for Growth priority areas.
- Notwithstanding the subdued reform pace, some bold actions have been taken – over one third of actions implemented in 2017 can be viewed as "major steps".
    - For example, Greece and Italy implemented major programmes to strengthen social protection, while France passed a long-overdue reform to improve the functioning of its labour market. Japan launched a new plan to significantly increase childcare capacity. Argentina passed a comprehensive tax reform.
- The intensity of reforms has also varied across policy areas:
    - Among reforms to boost skills acquisition and innovative capacity, actions taken to increase the size and efficiency of R&D support have been particularly widespread.
    - The bulk of actions taken to promote business dynamism and knowledge diffusion have focused on strengthening physical and legal infrastructure as well as on making product market regulation more competition-friendly.
    - A particularly high number of significant actions have been taken in the area of social benefits, which is important for social cohesion. To further help workers to cope with potentially rapid changes in jobs and tasks, more reforms are needed in complementary areas, such as improving active labour market and housing market policies to facilitate the job-market transition and mobility.
- A coherent reform strategy is crucial to reap synergies, manage trade-offs and ensure that the benefits are broadly shared over time.

1.1. Introduction

Global growth is on a broadly-based upturn. Advanced economies[1] are benefiting from rising investment and job creation, with unemployment already at pre-crisis levels in many countries and edging down in others. Emerging economies have seen their prospects improving with a rebound in some commodity markets and increases in public infrastructure investment. While encouraging, this short-term momentum should not obfuscate the longer-term challenges that need to be addressed in order to sustain improvements in living standards for all. Indeed, productivity growth – the main driver of long-term growth - continues to be weak in advanced economies and has slowed in many emerging-market economies. Business investment has increased in advanced economies, but still remains weaker than the average of past recoveries, implying that productive capital may not be growing fast enough. In emerging economies, enhanced capital deepening and productivity gains are necessary to escape the middle-income trap, to continue lifting millions out of poverty and to overcome demographic pressures.

Growth is still supported by favourable monetary conditions while in many countries private debt levels have remained elevated or further risen, which is not without risks to the outlook. An expanding majority of advanced economies have also finally closed the massive jobs gap that opened during the great recession, but not all segments of society are benefitting from the labour market recovery, with many youth and low-skilled workers still facing bleak job and career prospects. And despite rising employment, wages have largely failed to follow. In particular, real income growth has been weak at the bottom of the distribution, where the ground lost by the bottom 10% during the recession has still not been fully recovered (OECD, 2016a). Hence, translating the short-term recovery into strong and resilient long-term growth for all cannot be taken for granted.

Against this background, there is a strong case for ambitious structural reforms to move to robust and sustainable growth paths, with the gains shared by all. This chapter builds on the regular 2017 issue of *Going for Growth*, where priorities were set with a view to improving material living standards in an inclusive way through stronger employment and productivity gains. In essence, recommendations have been formulated with a view to pursuing three intertwined objectives:

Unlocking skills development and innovation capacity: Achieving stronger growth and reduced inequality requires action to better ensure that all individuals have the skills to obtain rewarding and productive employment and that these skills are put to their best use. Advances in digital technologies and the growing importance of knowledge-based capital underscore the need for reforms in education to ensure that young people are prepared for the dynamic labour market of the future and have the right cognitive and non-cognitive skills to cope with technological change. More efficient and effective policies to support innovation will help ensure these skills are turned into higher productivity growth.

Boosting business dynamism and diffusion of knowledge: To seek innovation and make the most of new technologies and workers' skills, firms must be given incentives to make the necessary investment in research and development (R&D), new digital equipment and organisational know-how. Strong product market competition and robust business dynamics – entry and growth, but also the exit of unproductive firms – are key for the diffusion of innovation and the allocation of resources to their best use. Businesses have a crucial role to play in fostering a good matching of skills and tasks by providing employment opportunities, contributing to skills development and knowledge diffusion.

Preserving social cohesion and helping workers make the most out of a dynamic labour market: Dealing with a rapid turnover of firms, jobs and tasks requires that workers facing a job loss be rapidly given new employment opportunities or a chance to up-grade skills, with adequate income support and job-search assistance during the transition. A well-functioning labour market, without unduly restrictive labour market regulation, and with appropriately designed unemployment benefits combined with comprehensive activation policies, will ensure that everyone can have access to jobs and labour market security. Such a job market will also be capable of better including population groups with thus far lower labour participation rates.

This chapter reviews the main growth challenges faced by advanced and emerging economies in pursuing these three objectives, and takes stock of actions taken that relate to policy recommendations on reform priorities laid out in the 2017 publication. It specifically evaluates the extent to which countries have already been addressing the 2017 reform priorities. The implementation of reforms is defined as the introduction of relevant laws and decrees or appropriate measures (such as budgetary provisions) put in place for the reform to come into effect. It cannot, however, evaluate how effectively those measures are enforced in practice. The next section presents a global overview of the reform momentum in 2017 compared to previous periods. The following section provides a brief reminder of the main performance challenges faced by countries. The final section reviews actions taken by countries across policy areas. An Annex provides the link to the online chapter on structural policy indicators, which contains a comprehensive cross-country set of quantitative policy indicators used in *Going for Growth*.

1.2. Overview of reform progress across countries

Reform activity, in advanced- and emerging-market economies alike, appears to be settling on a low level compared to the post-crisis peak. The number of reform actions in priority areas is also somewhat lower than what was observed before the crisis (OECD, 2017). On average across advanced economies, reforms have been fully implemented in 12% of the priority areas identified in the 2017 issue of *Going for Growth* (that is, relevant legislation or significant budgetary provisions have been passed for some recommendations in the priority areas). In addition, some reform action has been initiated (*i.e.* is in the process of implementation) in 35% of the areas (Figure 1.1). For emerging-market economies, the share of the *Going for Growth* priority areas where concrete actions have been taken remains lower than in advanced economies, with actions in the process of implementation in more than one fourth of priority areas.

Figure 1.1. Share of *Going for Growth* priority areas with actions taken

As a percentage of priorities, 2017

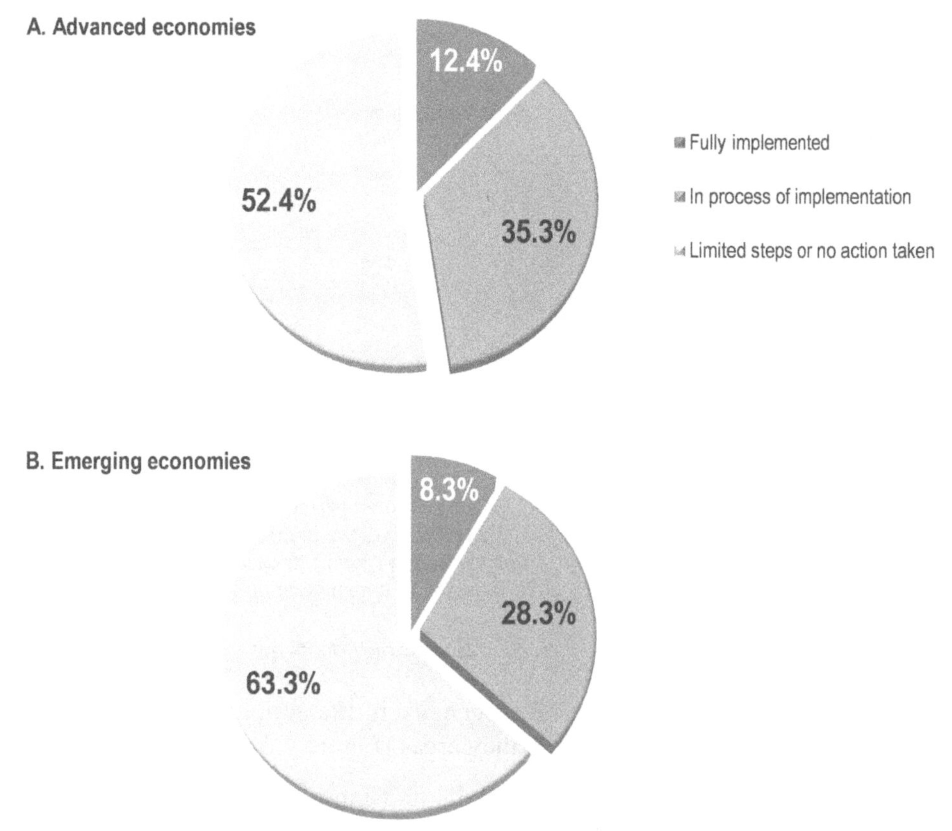

StatLink http://dx.doi.org/10.1787/888933680077

Reform intensity, as conveyed by the reform responsiveness rate indicator, looks set to remain below the peak observed in 2011-12. Considering jointly reforms fully implemented and in the process of implementation, the intensity has stabilised (Figure 1.2). Moreover, some bold actions were taken – over a third of actions implemented in 2017 have been assessed as "major steps" by OECD country specialists.[2] As legislative intensity can vary significantly from one year to the next – including due to political cycles - and the importance of individual actions can differ vastly, caution is needed in comparing the pace reported over the course of one year (2017) in this interim report relative to the pace averaged over a two year period (2015-16) documented in the previous issue of *Going for Growth.*

Figure 1.2. Despite the positive short-term prospects, reform intensity has stalled

Responsiveness rates to *Going for Growth* recommendations,[1] percentage

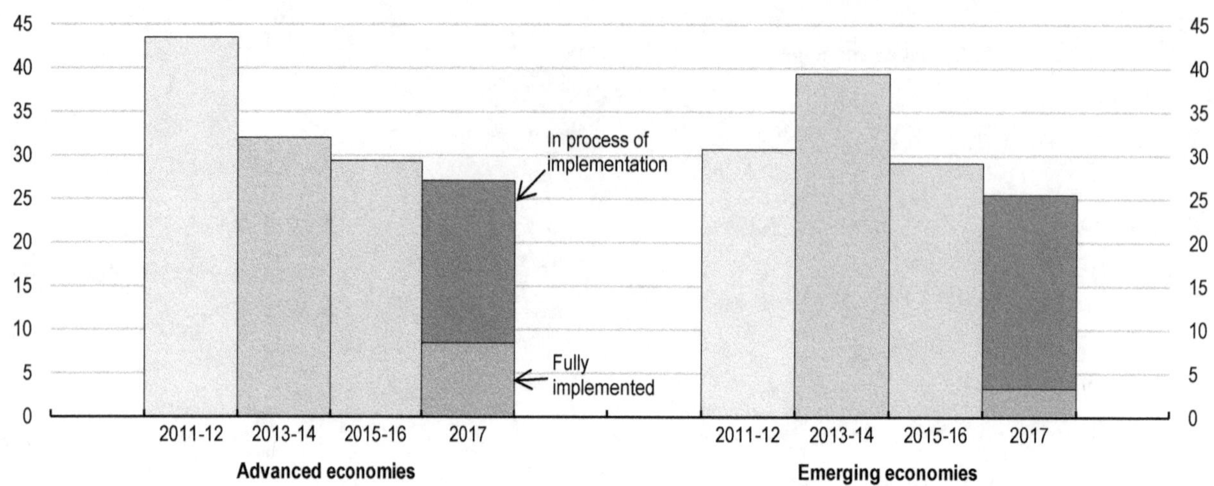

1. The chart illustrates the pace of reform in previous periods captured by the indicator of reform responsiveness (RRI) and the estimated level of responsiveness in 2017 based on fully implemented policies (red) and policy actions in the process of implementation (green) to ensure comparability with previous two-year periods. See the Going for Growth 2010 issue for an explanation on RRI.

StatLink http://dx.doi.org/10.1787/888933680096

This overall pattern hides some heterogeneity in the actions taken on *Going for Growth* recommendations across the main policy areas (Figure 1.3):

- Among the reforms to boost skills and innovative capacity, the largest share of actions implemented or in the process of implementation is observed in the areas of R&D investment and, to a lesser extent, higher education.
- Regarding the reforms that promote business dynamism and knowledge diffusion, the areas where most action is taking place are physical and legal infrastructure, with an emphasis on transportation networks, and the lowering of economy-wide regulatory barriers to competition, in particular in emerging-market economies.
- Among the reforms to enhance social cohesion and help workers to cope with potentially rapid changes in jobs and nature of tasks, social protection has seen an important share of actions taken, with significant anti-poverty programmes introduced in Italy and Greece. Priorities in the area of health care have also seen a relatively high share of reforms that have been fully implemented or in the process of implementation. In contrast, relatively few actions have been taken in the areas of labour taxation – an area where more substantial actions had been seen in 2015-16. The notable efforts to lift barriers to the participation of women in the labour force, which were reported in the previous issues of *Going for Growth,* have continued in 2017.

Figure 1.3. Reform intensity has been the highest in the area of social benefits, health and physical and legal infrastructure

Share of implemented recommendations,[1] percentage

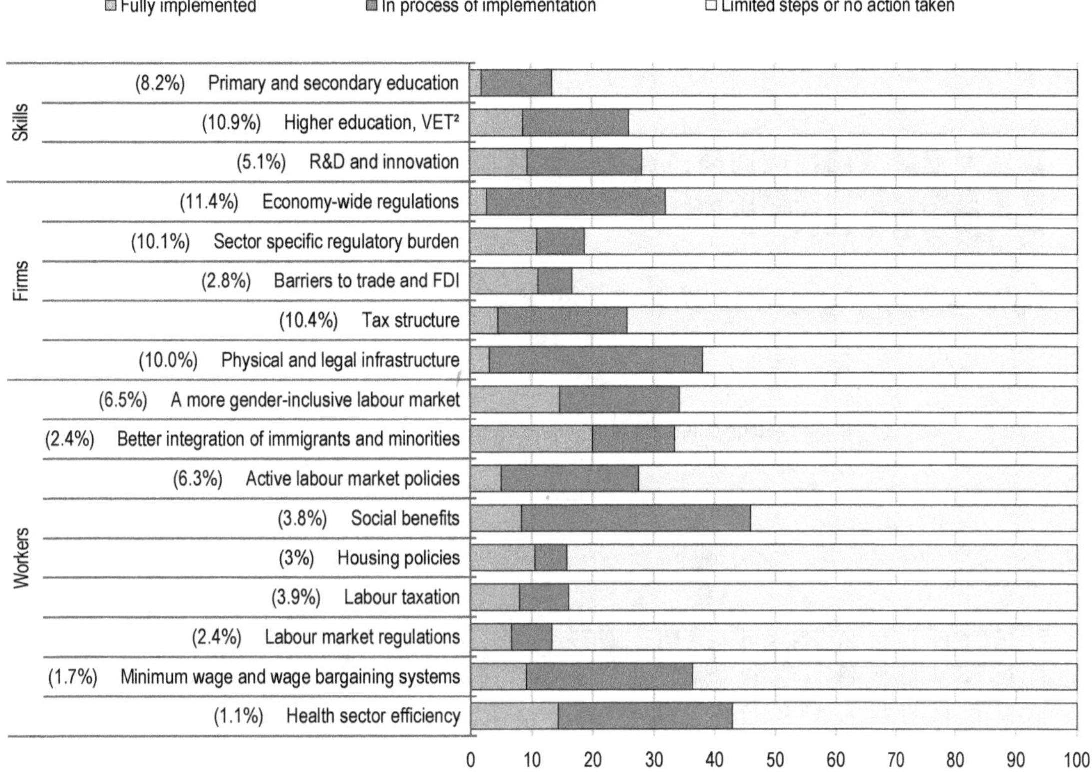

1. The chart summarises the share of recommendations made in Going for Growth 2017 by the status of their implementation. Full implementation refers to the adoption of relevant laws or equivalent measures. Values in parenthesis represent the share in total recommendations.
2. Vocational education and training.

StatLink http://dx.doi.org/10.1787/888933680115

1.3. Economic performance and Going for Growth 2017 reform priorities - a snapshot

Ensuring that the short-term momentum translates into strong long-term growth will require much more action than demonstrated in 2017. The policy priorities identified in the 2017 issue of *Going for Growth* remain valid and should continue to serve as guidance to a broadly-based structural reform agenda.

Going for Growth identifies policy reform priorities based on a 'mixed' approach combining a quantitative assessment that compares performances and policy indicators, and a qualitative assessment based on judgment and expertise provided by OECD country specialists. A standard overall benchmark is the average of top performing OECD countries on GDP per capita (Figure 1.4 and Figure 1.5). Priority reforms are identified even for those top performers based on weaknesses in specific areas and identified emerging challenges. The primary objective is to set a policy agenda most likely to secure long-term improvements in performance.

Figure 1.4. The sources of real income differences, advanced economies

Compared to the upper half of OECD countries, 2016[1]

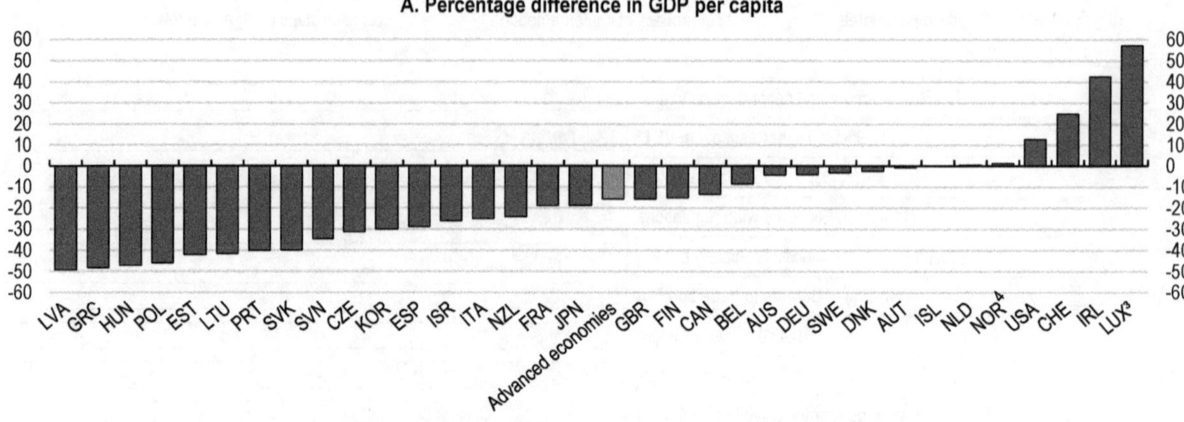

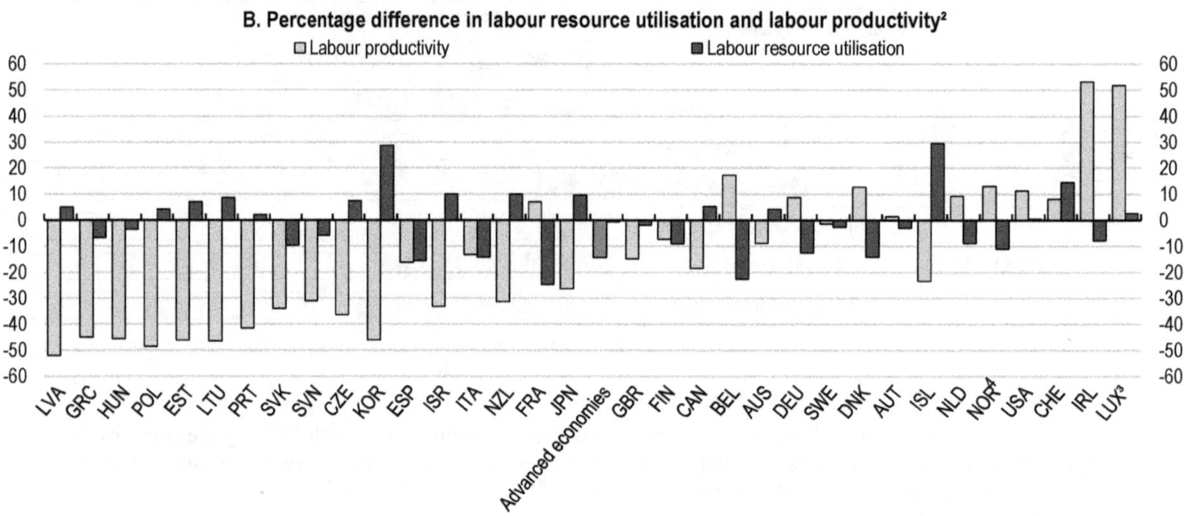

1. Compared to the weighted average using population weights of the 17 OECD countries with highest GDP per capita in 2016 based on 2016 purchasing power parities (PPPs). The sum of the percentage difference in labour resource utilisation and labour productivity do not add up exactly to the GDP per capita difference since the decomposition is multiplicative.
2. Labour productivity is measured as GDP per hour worked. Labour resource utilisation is measured as the total number of hours worked per capita.
3. In the case of Luxembourg, the population is augmented by the number of cross-border workers in order to take into account their contribution to GDP.
4. Data refer to GDP for mainland Norway which excludes petroleum production and shipping. While total GDP overestimates the sustainable income potential, mainland GDP slightly underestimates it since returns on the financial assets held by the petroleum fund abroad are not included.

Source: OECD, National Accounts, Productivity, Employment Outlook and Economic Outlook Databases.

StatLink http://dx.doi.org/10.1787/888933680134

Figure 1.5. The sources of real income differences, emerging economies

Compared to the upper half of OECD countries, 2016[1]

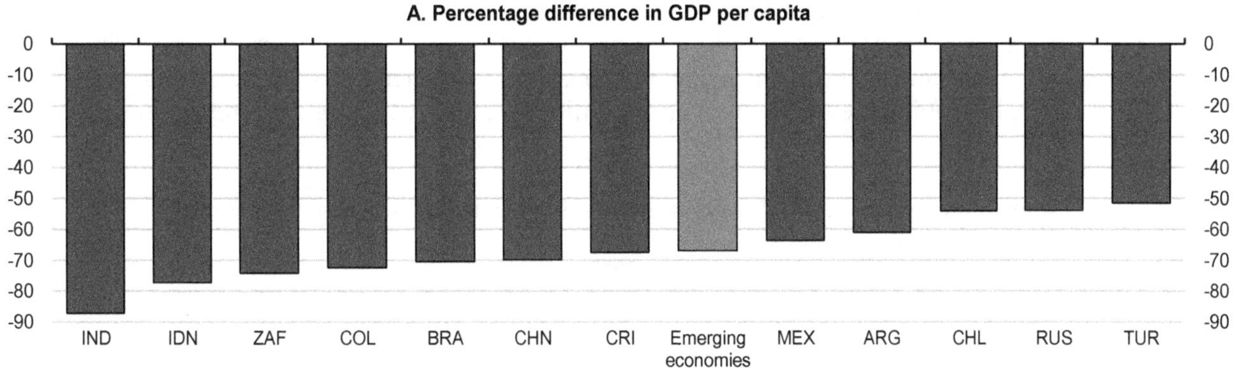

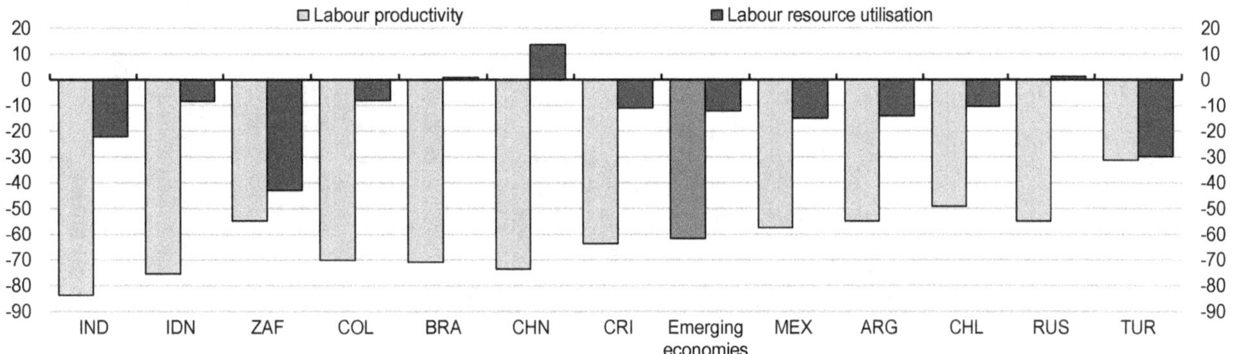

1. Compared to the weighted average using population weights of the 17 OECD countries with highest GDP per capita in 2016 based on 2016 purchasing power parities (PPPs). The sum of the percentage difference in labour resource utilisation and labour productivity do not add up exactly to the GDP per capita difference since the decomposition is multiplicative.

2. Labour productivity is measured as GDP per employee. Labour resource utilisation is measured as employment as a share of population.

Source: OECD National Accounts and Productivity Databases; World Bank, World Development Indicators (WDI) (Database); ILO (International Labour Organisation), Key Indicators of the Labour Market (KILM) Database for employment data on Brazil, Colombia, Indonesia; Statistics South Africa for employment data on South Africa; India National Sample Survey (various years), annual population estimates from the Registrar General and OECD estimates for employment data on India; China Ministry of Human Resources and Social Security for employment data on China.

StatLink http://dx.doi.org/10.1787/888933680153

As the job market situation improves - due to a combination of a cyclical pick-up and actions taken on past employment-related priorities - the medium-term policy preoccupation is more with the slowdown in productivity growth and the pass-through from technological leaders to a broader population of firms. Hence, the bulk of 2017 policy priorities, in particular in advanced countries, concern promoting business dynamism and knowledge diffusion (labelled 'firms' in Figure 1.6). Most common areas include sector-specific and economy-wide regulations with an emphasis on professional services and retail distribution, as well as the streamlining of licensing and permits.

Other priorities include shifting the tax burden from direct sources (labour and capital income) to indirect sources (taxes on consumption, immovable property and pollution emissions) while broadening the tax base, enhancing connectivity in transport and improving the efficiency of public administration. For emerging economies, priorities to boost business dynamism and knowledge diffusion account for an even larger share of total priorities (around half), and primarily include streamlining permits, lowering barriers to trade and investment, expanding regulatory impact assessment, setting one-stop shops, improving the quality and accessibility of infrastructure and strengthening the rule of law.

Figure 1.6. Distribution of *Going for Growth* priorities across broad categories

2017

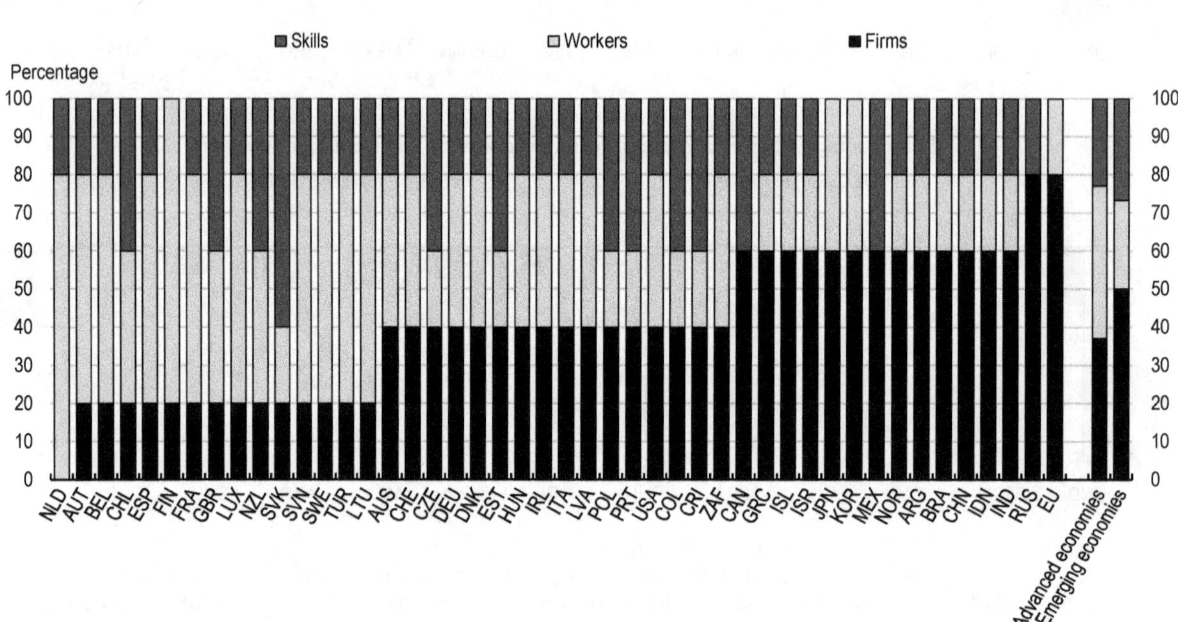

StatLink http://dx.doi.org/10.1787/888933680172

Priorities focussing on helping current and future workers to acquire or improve their skills and on increasing the overall innovative capacity of the economy also largely address the productivity slowdown, but with an important inclusiveness angle – aiming for longer-term growth to benefit all. Across advanced economies, a quarter of priorities fall in this area, but they dominate in the Slovak Republic, while being significant in Canada, Czech Republic, Estonia, New Zealand, Poland, Portugal and the United Kingdom (labelled "skills" in Figure 1.6). Roughly 80% of the skills' priorities concern the need to reform education, with better support to disadvantaged students, improving teaching quality, vocational education and training (VET), and expanding long-life learning having the largest occurrences. Priorities on R&D and innovation follow. In emerging economies, the emphasis on education is similar – with roughly 80% of priorities in skills linked to higher vocational education and training, as well as primary and secondary education.

Finally, priorities to help workers cope with and adapt to job and task changes and promote social cohesion focus primarily on how to facilitate access and attachment to the labour market (labelled "workers" in Figure 1.6). Particular attention is given to groups with traditionally lower participation and employment rates and higher risks of falling out of the labour market: women, minorities, youth, the low-skilled, the disabled and the elderly. In other words, emphasis is placed on policies that have the largest scope to make growth more inclusive. Countries having the most important gaps in labour utilisation generally have a high share of priorities in 'workers' (Belgium, France, Spain and Turkey – Figure 1.6). Some countries with a relatively high level of income inequality, as measured by the Gini coefficient (Figure 1.7) are among those with a lower share of priorities in the category 'workers' (Brazil, China, Costa Rica, India and Mexico). In total, over a third of priorities for advanced economies can be classified in the category labelled 'workers' (Figure 1.6), of which more than half focus on implicit and explicit barriers to employment and labour force participation, as well as activation policies. In emerging-market economies, the share of priorities in the category 'workers' is lower, focusing mainly on unemployment and social benefits, labour market regulations and tax wedges.

Figure 1.7. Inequality remains a challenge, particularly in developing economies

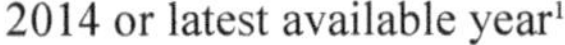
2014 or latest available year[1]

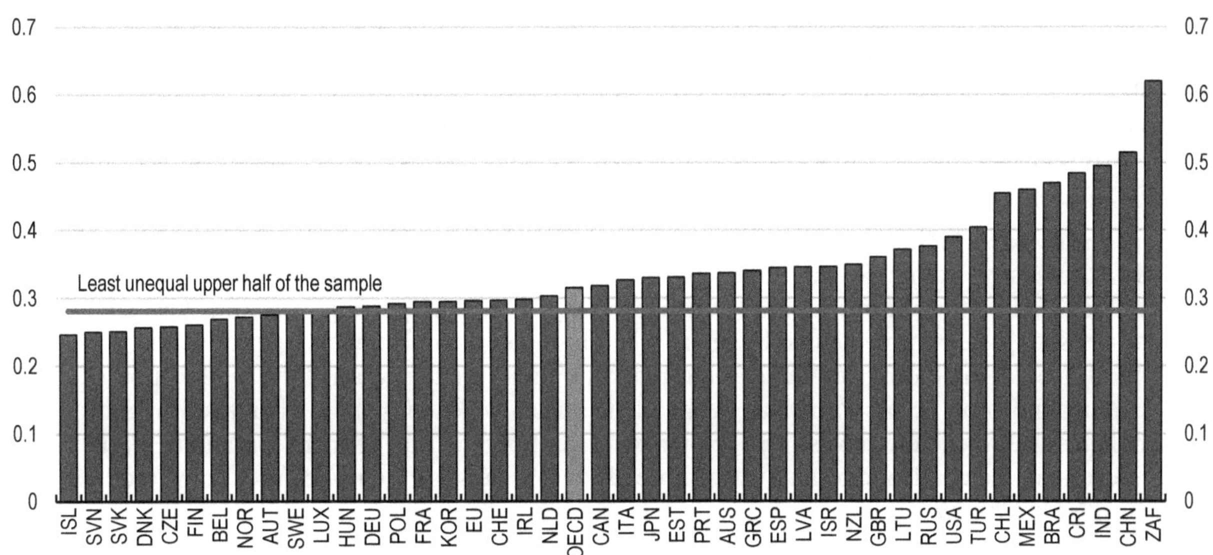

1. Gini at disposable income (after taxes and transfers), for total population. The latest available year is 2016 for Costa Rica; 2015 for Chile, Finland, the United Kingdom, Israel, Korea, the Netherlands, the United States, South Africa; 2013 for Brazil and China; 2011 for India and the Russian Federation.
Source: OECD, Income Distribution Database.

StatLink http://dx.doi.org/10.1787/888933680191

Importantly, the three categories "firms", "skills" and "workers" should not be seen in isolation. To enhance the effectiveness of reforms and ensure that their benefits are shared broadly – but also to enhance their social and political acceptability – a coherent reform strategy is crucial. As advocated in *Going for Growth* 2017, such a strategy can be most beneficial if formulated as (explicit or implicit) reform packages – combining various policy reforms within and across the categories, in order to reap synergies, manage trade-offs and improve the distribution of effects over time. For example, reforms to stimulate business dynamism – such as reducing barriers to firm entry and exit - should be accompanied by labour market measures to help vulnerable workers transition to new jobs. The new dynamism and innovative activity generated by such reforms will likely accelerate the transformation of tasks and skills requirements – highlighting the need for actions in education policies, which can take a longer time to materialise.

1.4. Progress in unlocking skills development and innovation for all

Knowledge is likely to be the main driver of growth in the future and policies geared towards enhancing skills for all will be crucial in this respect. Improving education and skills has always been identified as a priority for a vast majority of advanced and emerging economies and the specific recommendations vary depending on the sources of policy weaknesses. But despite widespread and sustained reform action over the years, they usually fall short of fully addressing country-specific skills priorities, which often appear from one to the next issue of *Going for Growth*. Indeed, education and skills priorities often require pursued efforts and monitoring of actions over an extended period of time.

Education is also an essential driver of an economy's innovative capacity. A strong network of knowledge transmission nurtured through R&D collaboration among firms, as well as between higher education institutes and firms, is conducive to innovation-led growth. A highly qualified labour force is essential for the adoption of ideas and turning them into improvements in production. And, providing a larger share of firms, in particular smaller and younger firms, with access to sources of knowledge and advanced skills can help bridge the dispersion between leading, frontier firms and those lagging behind (Andrews et al., 2015), making productivity growth more inclusive.

The success of the match between education and innovation relies on a broader range of assets, mostly intangible: employee skills, organisational know-how, databases, design, brands and various forms of intellectual property. Policies spurring investment in such assets should be complemented by appropriate framework conditions, *e.g.* product, labour and financial (including venture capital) market policies that encourage the reallocation of capital and jobs across firms, as well as effective bankruptcy laws that keep a good balance between the costs and benefits of entrepreneurial experimentation. Thus, addressing the challenge of innovation spreads across most of the policy areas covered by *Going for Growth.*

1.4.1. Reforms to foster primary and secondary education

In primary and secondary education, a common emphasis is on raising teachers' qualifications and addressing educational inequalities, and enhancing the targeting and effectiveness of resources devoted to disadvantaged students and schools (Table 1.1). Indeed, social returns to education are high, but relate mostly to earlier stages of education, especially for disadvantaged individuals (Heckman et al., 2005). Increasing the quality of lower-level schooling across broad segments of the population is thus important for securing improved productivity but also for fostering inclusiveness, notably by achieving rising participation in higher education. High-quality primary and secondary education should be prioritised in public funding because those are a prerequisite for raising skill levels and expanding tertiary education. For emerging-market countries, recommendations to address bottlenecks in schooling infrastructure are relatively frequent, which may require raising public investment. Recent actions in this area include:

- France halved class size to 12 pupils for grade 1 and grade 2 in poor neighbourhoods, with implementation already started during the 2017-18 school year.
- Mexico finalised the implementation of the mandated National Evaluation System of teachers, where almost all of the teaching body has been evaluated, and public investment has been undertaken to improve schools' infrastructure.
- Sweden increased appropriations targeted to schools with weak results, and to upper-secondary education for pupils without the grades to directly integrate the standard programmes.

Table 1.1. Recommendations and actions in primary and secondary education

	Provide additional support to disadvantaged schools/students	Improve teaching quality and teachers career prospects/ incentives	Postpone early tracking	Limit grade repetition	Improve school accountability and autonomy	Improve access/ enrolment	Provide second chance opportunities
Australia							
Austria							
Belgium							
Canada							
Czech Republic							
Denmark							
Estonia							
EU							
Finland							
France							
Germany							
Greece							
Hungary							
Iceland							
Ireland							
Israel							
Italy							
Japan							
Korea							
Latvia							
Lithuania							
Luxembourg							
Netherlands							
Norway							
New Zealand							
Poland							
Portugal							
Slovak Republic							
Slovenia							
Spain							
Sweden							
Switzerland							
United Kingdom							
United States							
Argentina							
Brazil							
Chile							
China							
Colombia							
Costa Rica							
Indonesia							
India							
Mexico							
Russia							
South Africa							
Turkey							

Note: Blue cells represent recommendations for a given country in a given area (with no action taken in 2017). Maroon cells represent actions taken on a recommendation (fully implemented or in the process of implementation).

1.4.2. Reforms to expand higher and vocational education and training

Recommendations in the area of tertiary education are more prevalent for higher-income countries, with a common challenge to improve university responsiveness to labour market needs (Table 1.2). Indeed, digitalisation, globalisation, demographic shifts and other changes in work organisation are constantly reshaping skill needs (OECD, 2016b). Excess inertia in the education and training systems, in particular in universities, translates into people acquiring inadequate skills and eventually into persistent skill shortages and mismatches. The latter are costly for individuals, firms and society in terms of lower wages, productivity and growth. Flexibility and the ability to equip students with skills enabling them to more rapid adaptation to task changes are thus vital. Similarly, recommendations in the area of vocational education and training (VET) also aim at responding to the challenge of aligning of skills with labour market needs. Expanding or enhancing the effectiveness of VET will provide a better bridge between education and the labour market. This is needed as the nature of future economic growth will likely entail substantial firm turnover (OECD, 2015). As a result, policies should focus on facilitating job matching, allowing the labour force to adapt more quickly to new skill requirements and changes in industrial and occupational structures. Recent actions in this area include:

- Colombia has launched the Access and Quality in Higher Education Project (PACES), with the aim of improving the quality of higher education and tackling inequality of access through the use of loans for disadvantaged students. Education loans have also been reformed to eliminate caps on loans and ease access to accredited universities for poorer students.
- Germany has simplified procedures and improved financial support for individuals pursuing life-long learning as well as for vocational education graduates. Moreover, universities have received additional funding to support studies, in particular for students from vocational education pathways. Measures to improve the school-to-work transition, including job counselling, have also been reinforced.
- Latvia has developed a modular VET curriculum that provides training programmes tailored for specific skill needs for each industry. It also introduced a legal framework for work-based learning and raised the fiscal incentives to undertake VET by partially exempting students' earnings from the income tax. VET schools have been consolidated and VET Competence Centres which experiment with new curricula and offer adult education were established.
- In the United Kingdom, spending on lifelong learning pilots has been increased in England to test different approaches to help workers retrain and upskill throughout their adult lives. The pilots will inform a wider National Retraining Scheme, which is set to be introduced in England. VET qualifications are also going to be modified to simplify the technical education system.

Table 1.2. Recommendations and actions in higher education, vocational education and training

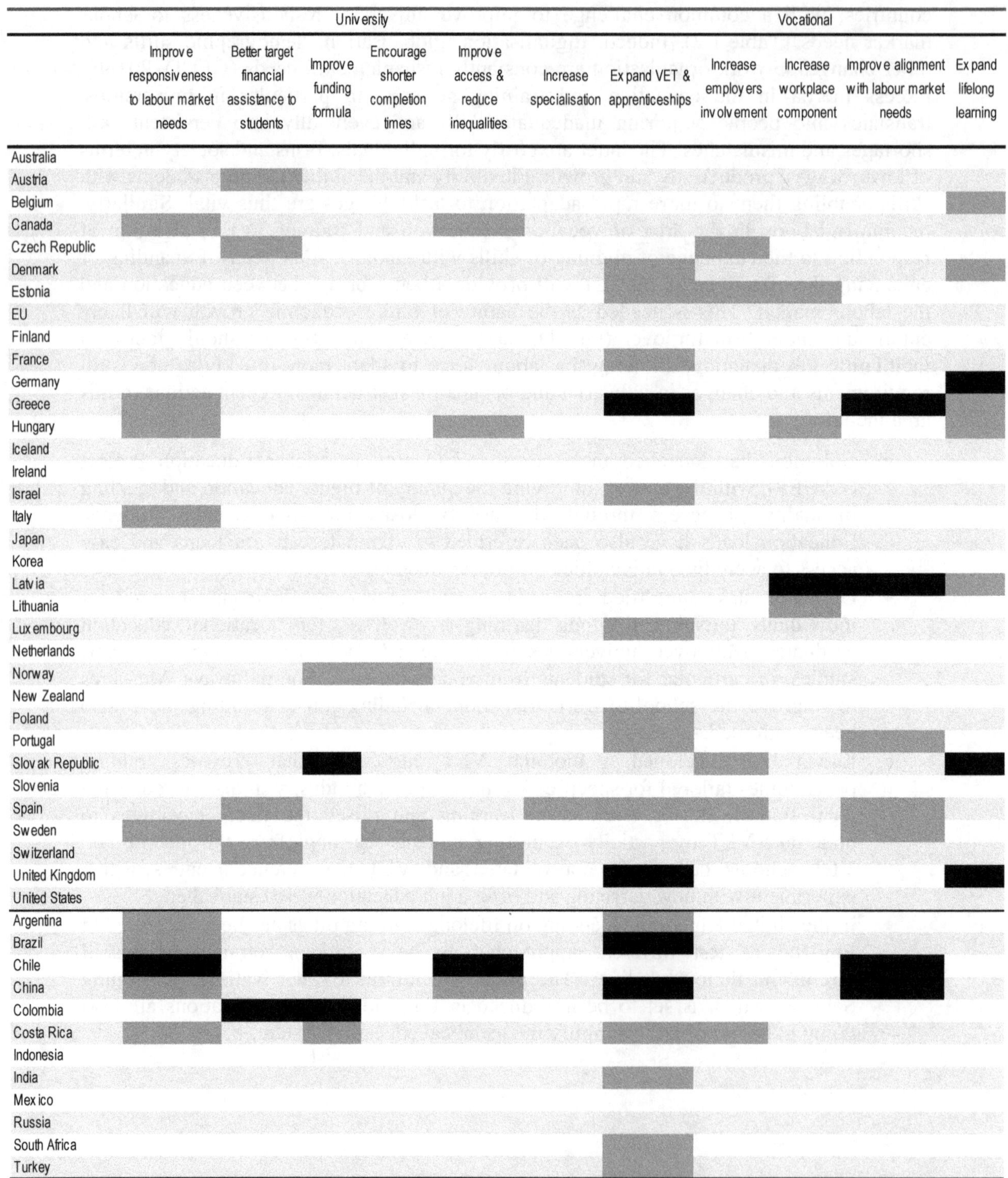

	University						Vocational				
	Improve responsiveness to labour market needs	Better target financial assistance to students	Improve funding formula	Encourage shorter completion times	Improve access & reduce inequalities	Increase specialisation	Expand VET & apprenticeships	Increase employers involvement	Increase workplace component	Improve alignment with labour market needs	Expand lifelong learning
Australia											
Austria											
Belgium											
Canada											
Czech Republic											
Denmark											
Estonia											
EU											
Finland											
France											
Germany											
Greece											
Hungary											
Iceland											
Ireland											
Israel											
Italy											
Japan											
Korea											
Latvia											
Lithuania											
Luxembourg											
Netherlands											
Norway											
New Zealand											
Poland											
Portugal											
Slovak Republic											
Slovenia											
Spain											
Sweden											
Switzerland											
United Kingdom											
United States											
Argentina											
Brazil											
Chile											
China											
Colombia											
Costa Rica											
Indonesia											
India											
Mexico											
Russia											
South Africa											
Turkey											

Note: Blue cells represent recommendations for a given country in a given area (with no action taken in 2017). Maroon cells represent actions taken on a recommendation (fully implemented or in the process of implementation).

1.4.3. Reforms to improve innovation capacity

In both advanced and emerging economies, recommendations on innovation include generally strengthening collaboration between research institutes or universities and industry. Efficient public support to R&D also remains warranted, as investing in innovation involves considerable uncertainty while associated outcomes often have some public good qualities - being widely shared within the economy and even abroad. A mix of incremental R&D tax incentives and selective direct grants is considered the best approach, with recommendations focusing on achieving a better balance between the two types of support and pursuing close evaluation of the grant programmes (Table 1.3). Recent actions in this area include:

- The Czech Republic passed a new evaluation methodology to improve the effectiveness of spending in R&D.
- Estonia substantially increased the weight of business contracts in the funding formula for public research institutions.
- Mexico introduced a new tax credit regime for R&D – making 30% of an increase in R&D expenses and investments (with respect to past values) deductible from taxes.
- The Netherlands extended the scheme to subsidise labour and other costs associated with undertaking R&D.

Table 1.3. Recommendations and actions in R&D

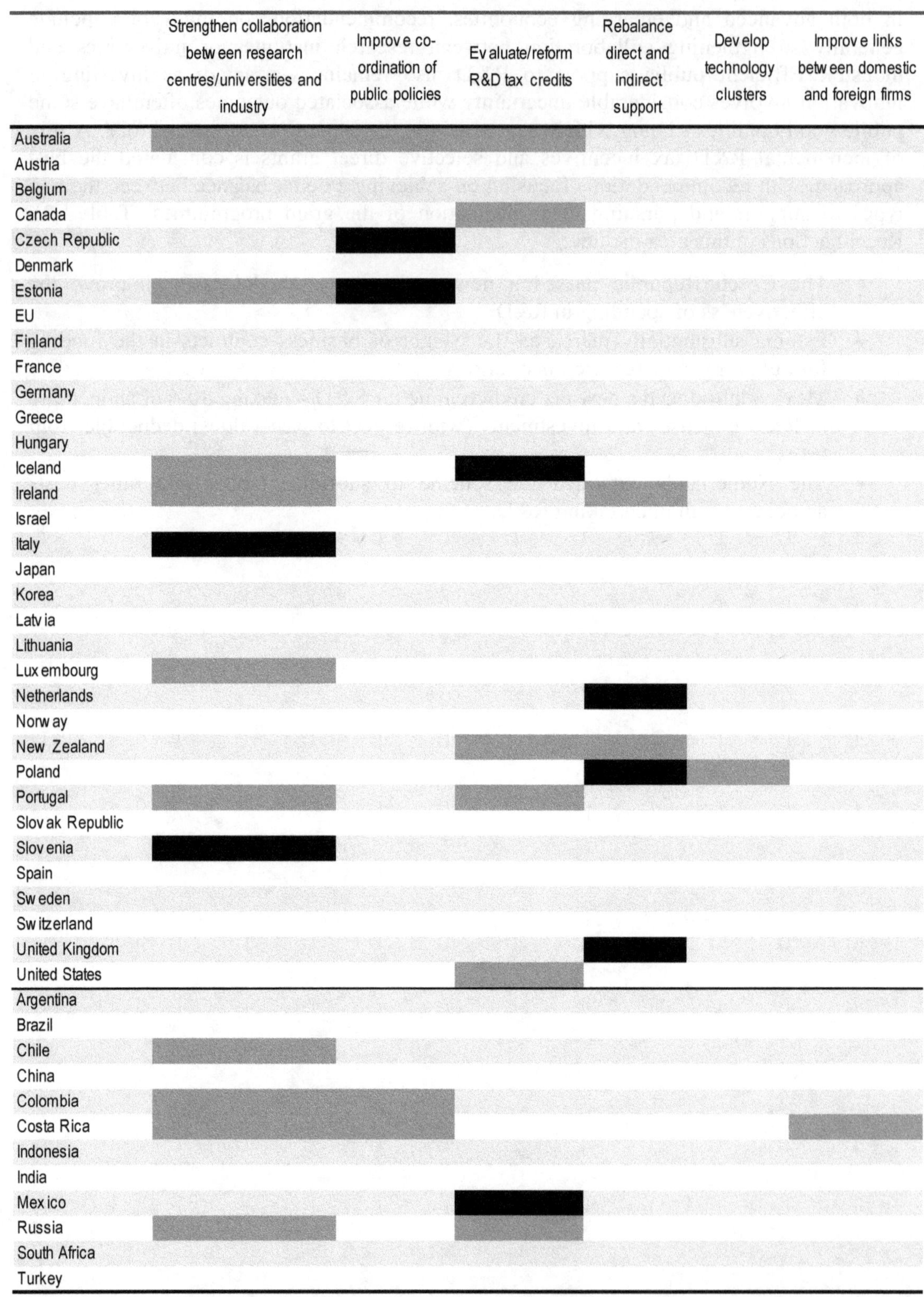

	Strengthen collaboration between research centres/universities and industry	Improve co-ordination of public policies	Evaluate/reform R&D tax credits	Rebalance direct and indirect support	Develop technology clusters	Improve links between domestic and foreign firms
Australia						
Austria						
Belgium						
Canada						
Czech Republic						
Denmark						
Estonia						
EU						
Finland						
France						
Germany						
Greece						
Hungary						
Iceland						
Ireland						
Israel						
Italy						
Japan						
Korea						
Latvia						
Lithuania						
Luxembourg						
Netherlands						
Norway						
New Zealand						
Poland						
Portugal						
Slovak Republic						
Slovenia						
Spain						
Sweden						
Switzerland						
United Kingdom						
United States						
Argentina						
Brazil						
Chile						
China						
Colombia						
Costa Rica						
Indonesia						
India						
Mexico						
Russia						
South Africa						
Turkey						

Note: Blue cells represent recommendations for a given country in a given area (with no action taken in 2017). Maroon cells represent actions taken on a recommendation (fully implemented or in the process of implementation).

1.5. Progress in boosting business dynamism and faster diffusion of knowledge

Recent decades have seen a persistent and worrying slowdown in productivity growth, which is a central driver of long-term improvements in living standards. More recently, the slowdown has extended to emerging economies. Slower productivity growth is fuelling concerns of low global long-term growth, amid population ageing. Recent evidence has characterised this slowdown in productivity growth as a reflection of both cyclical and structural factors, which have – thus far – prevented rapid technological changes from translating into aggregate productivity gains as it has done in the past. One major factor, which is part cyclical but to some extent also structural, has been persistently weak investment in physical capital (Ollivaud et al., 2016): in most advanced countries, the recovery in non-residential investment is lagging behind that of GDP, and this is particularly the case among European countries. But behind the aggregate slowdown, there has been also a growing dispersion of productivity performance within countries between firms and regions, with some of them enjoying fast productivity gains enabled by rapid technological progress, and others lagging behind. In other words, while the productivity frontier keeps advancing, these gains have not diffused throughout the rest of the economy (Andrews et al., 2016).

The role of businesses is crucial in addressing these challenges. They can provide employment opportunities, contribute to skills development and engage in knowledge and technology diffusion, which is particularly important for emerging economies. But this requires a business environment that encourages them to do so and ensures a level playing field so that they can compete on ideas and business models. Policy makers need to deploy a range of policies that i) enable firms to invest in breakthrough innovation, ii) ease firm access to skilled workers, finance, and markets to experiment with new ideas and capitalise on them to grow, iii) support the diffusion of innovation throughout the economy and across the world, thus enabling all firms to benefit from these innovations and grow, and iv) allow for the smooth exit of unproductive firms to free up valuable resources, including workers, so that they can contribute to more rewarding activities.

Achieving these policy objectives will span many areas from competition and product market regulation to innovation and financial market policies. The *Going for Growth* framework identifies such country-specific priorities to be implemented at the national level. Globalisation - closer economic integration and rising cross-country interdependence - brings additional challenges that require stronger international co-ordination on structural policies in a number of areas, not only trade but also R&D, the protection of intellectual property rights, taxation, competition and other fields affecting the corporate sector.

1.5.1. Reforms to economy-wide and sector-specific regulations to facilitate firms' entry and exit

Pro-competition product market regulations affect aggregate productivity via various channels such as the speed at which new sectors can grow, the incentives for innovative efforts and the adoption of new technologies, as well as the capacity of the economy to allocate capital and labour resources to their best use. In emerging economies, high regulatory burdens can also act as a barrier to business formalisation. Estimates of the potential impacts of product market reform point to a strong pay-off, with gains in living standards achieved relatively rapidly (Egert and Gal, 2017). Additionally, recent empirical evidence suggests that pro-competition product market reforms can be inclusive in that they tend to lift household incomes across the distribution, leaving inequality broadly unchanged (Causa et al., 2016). At the economy-wide level, reducing the regulatory burden is needed in many countries. Frequent associated recommendations include streamlining regulation while facilitating firm entry through simplified and transparent permit and licence procedures, reducing the scope of state-owned enterprises while improving their governance, and strengthening competition frameworks (Table 1.4). Recent actions in this area include:

- Hungary passed a new legislation to significantly increase merger notification thresholds. Furthermore, the EU's antitrust damage directive was adopted, making it easier for injured parties to obtain compensation for damages due to anticompetitive conduct.
- Chile is rolling out its 2020 digital agenda to increase e-procedures for households and firms. Moreover, 40 municipalities are currently experimenting "Escritorio Empresa", a digital platform to simplify firm procedures.
- Latvia passed an action plan for the improvement of the business environment. Measures include on-line registration of a company starting from 2018 and the registration of property without a notary but with a safe electronic signature.

Table 1.4. Recommendations and actions to lift regulatory distortions and promote firms' entry and exit

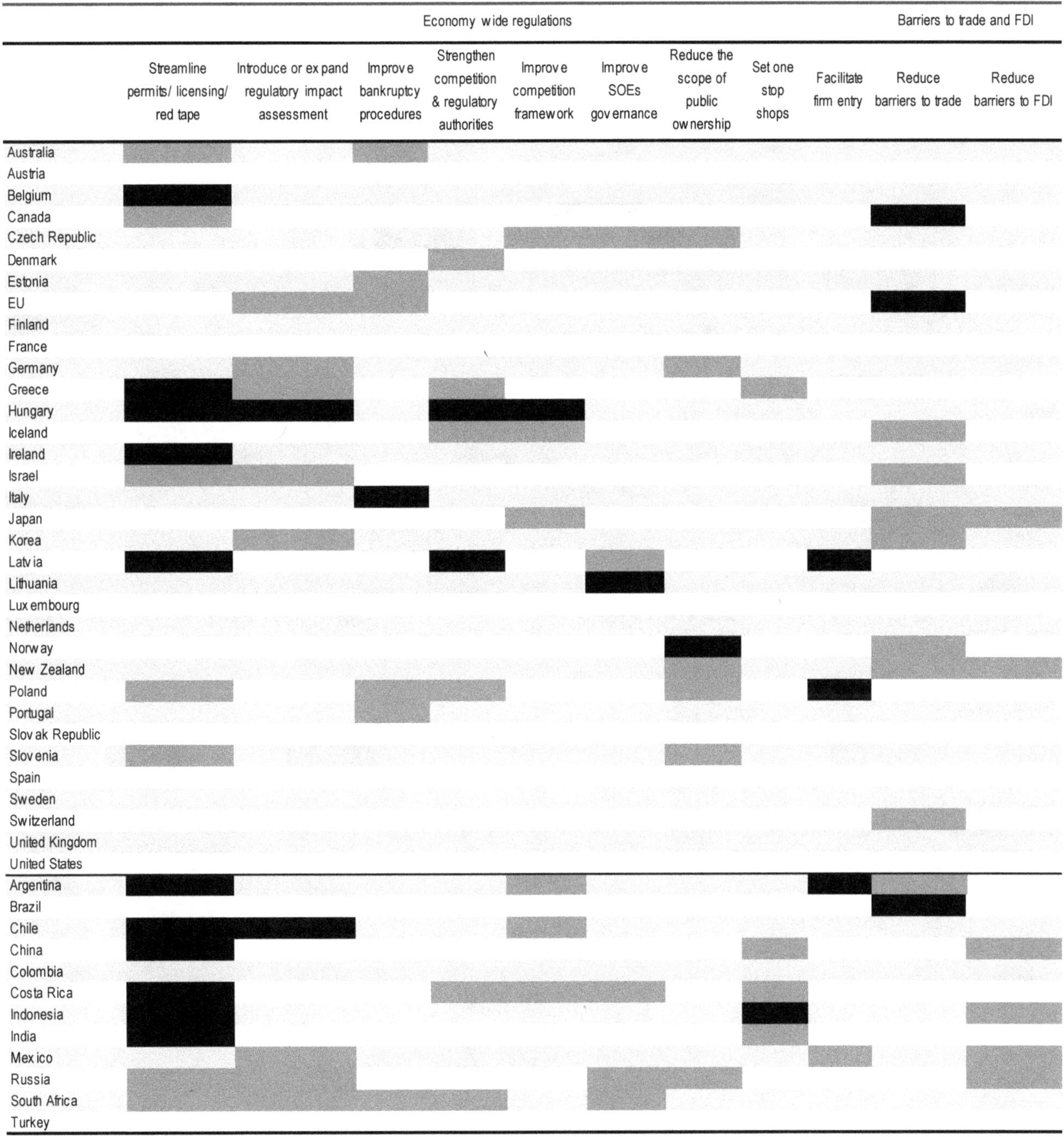

Note: Blue cells represent recommendations for a given country in a given area (with no action taken in 2017). Maroon cells represent actions taken on a recommendation (fully implemented or in the process of implementation).

Table 1.5. Recommendations and actions to lift sector specific regulatory burdens

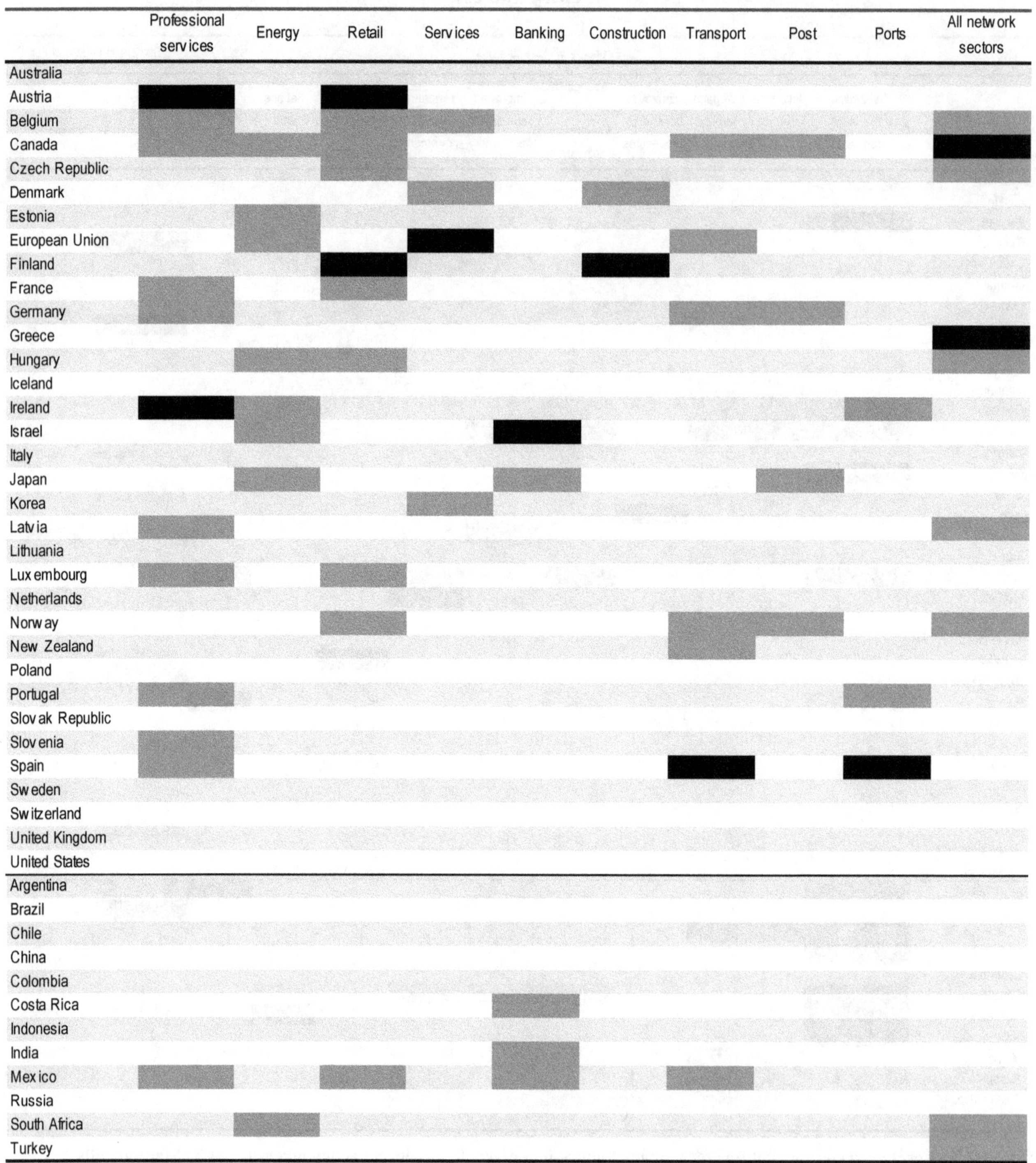

	Professional services	Energy	Retail	Services	Banking	Construction	Transport	Post	Ports	All network sectors
Australia										
Austria										
Belgium										
Canada										
Czech Republic										
Denmark										
Estonia										
European Union										
Finland										
France										
Germany										
Greece										
Hungary										
Iceland										
Ireland										
Israel										
Italy										
Japan										
Korea										
Latvia										
Lithuania										
Luxembourg										
Netherlands										
Norway										
New Zealand										
Poland										
Portugal										
Slovak Republic										
Slovenia										
Spain										
Sweden										
Switzerland										
United Kingdom										
United States										
Argentina										
Brazil										
Chile										
China										
Colombia										
Costa Rica										
Indonesia										
India										
Mexico										
Russia										
South Africa										
Turkey										

Note: Blue cells represent recommendations for a given country in a given area (with no action taken in 2017). Maroon cells represent actions taken on a recommendation (fully implemented or in the process of implementation).

Reducing sector-specific regulatory burdens, especially in non-manufacturing, i.e. retail trade and professional services as well as network industries, are also frequent recommendations (Table 1.5). Product market reforms in this area could facilitate adjustments in unit labour costs in a context of low inflation. Furthermore, reducing regulatory barriers to firm entry and competition in sectors where there is pent-up demand such as retail trade and professional services can spur job creation. Stronger competition, especially in services, would help to ensure productivity gains mainly translate into wage increases and that workers' real income also benefit from lower consumer prices. This would help workers to reap the benefits from previously-introduced labour market reforms. In fact, product market reforms have become even more important now insofar as the lack of competition in some product markets risks undermining the success of previous labour market liberalisation reforms. Recent actions in this area include:

- Costa Rica simplified the registration procedure of low-risk food and cosmetic products, and implemented pilot projects with municipalities to streamline licensing.
- A Services package to tackle barriers in the services market was adopted by the European Commission. It includes (i) a legislative proposal establishing a new notification procedure for services under the Services Directive, (ii) a guidance on specific reform needs per country, (iii) an analytical framework for proportionality analysis ("the proportionality test") in order to assist Member States in targeting instances of disproportionate and unnecessary regulation, (iv) a legislative proposal introducing the European Services card, which aims at facilitating the cross-border exercise of a number of activities in the area of services. The proposals will facilitate the mobility of professionals and streamline the administrative procedure that EU business service providers have to follow to expand their activities to other EU countries.
- Ireland simplified the licensing procedures to start a business by creating the Integrated Licence Application Service (ILAS).
- Spain adopted some measures to ease the implementation of the Market Unity Law.

Policies that promote efficient firm entry and exit are regularly featured in *Going for Growth* (Table 1.4). Pushing out the production frontier requires enabling experimentation with new technologies and business models. Since new firms are often the vehicle through which such new technologies and business practices enter the market, the policy framework should be conducive to firm entry while framework conditions need to ensure that innovative new firms can get a foothold in the market. Recent evidence suggests that the policy environment often favour incumbents over start-ups (Calvino et al., 2016). In some cases policies and regulations – introduced for good reasons, such as consumer and environmental protection - can unintentionally serve as barriers to the entry of new technologies and business practices. In many cases such negative design features can be avoided or minimised. However, the policy environment should not only encourage the entry of new firms and enable them to grow, but it should also encourage unsuccessful firms to close down. In the case of a start-up, a failure needs to be recognised as an opportunity for the entrepreneur to learn and rebound, to find new opportunities which lead to more rapid growth, and thus to create new employment opportunities. This in turn facilitates more effective knowledge diffusion. In practical terms, this calls for bankruptcy legislation that does not excessively penalise business failure (see also Chapter 3). Recent actions in this area include:

- Argentina legislated a new entrepreneurship law to reduce barriers on start-ups.
- Latvia created a monitoring system of insolvency proceedings.
- Poland passed a set of reforms (Constitution for Business) to ease the starting, running and ending of business operations.

Greater openness to trade and foreign direct investment (FDI) opens access to global demand for and supply of goods, services, technologies and knowledge. It boosts competition and knowledge spill-overs (Andrews and Cingano, 2012) and facilitates participation in Global Value Chains (GVCs). However, GVCs can actually increase the negative impacts of tariff and non-tariff trade barriers, as goods and services cross borders multiple times (OECD, 2013) – strengthening the case to reduce such barriers. Recommendations in this area cover tariff and especially non-tariff barriers, which remain of particular concern, both in general as well as in specific sectors. No significant progress has been made on trade and investment barriers, though Brazil has scaled back some local content requirements in fossil fuel investment projects.

Inefficient subsidies such as to energy and agricultural production have adverse effects on the efficiency of resource allocation and can increase pressure on the natural environment. While reducing such subsidies is a long-standing priority in several advanced countries and at the EU level, no progress has been made in 2017. However, in emerging economies, Argentina has undertaken significant efforts to reduce fossil fuel subsidies.

1.5.2. Reforms to make the tax system more friendly to growth

There is solid evidence of the impact of the tax structure on economic growth, through effects not only on labour utilisation (see above) but also private investment and productivity (Arnold et al., 2011). A more growth- and equity-friendly tax system can be achieved by shifting the tax burden toward immovable property, broadening the tax base and reducing the fragmentation of the tax system. A shift to environmental taxation can also help improve the sustainability of growth and well-being, provided measures are taken to ensure that lower-income households are not disproportionately impacted by green taxes. The pace of reform in this area has been slowing recently across advanced economies, following a period of widespread crisis-driven tax reforms. Countries still exhibit wide scope for improvement in this respect, and tax reform features among frequent priorities. Recommendations vary depending on country-specific performance and policy weaknesses (Table 1.6). Reductions in labour or corporate taxes are generally recommended alongside increases in indirect taxes; whether it is recommended to increase one or several of these taxes depends on country-specific sources of policy distortions. Moreover, striking the right balance may be challenging - the scope for such reforms may be limited in some cases, as they may increase inequality (Causa et al., 2016). Recent actions in this area include:

- Argentina has broadened the tax base in the personal income tax as capital income will start to be taxed, which will increase progressivity. Moreover, a reduction in employers' social security contributions for low-skilled workers will encourage formalisation. The reform will also reduce corporate tax rates from 35% to 25% for reinvested profits.
- In Canada, the Federal budget eliminated a number of inefficient tax measures and removed some tax expenditures to improve consistency.
- Denmark initiated a property tax reform to link tax payments to house price developments and to create a new system for property valuation.
- Greece improved tax compliance and lowered the tax-free threshold on personal income by a third, effective 2020.
- Italy undertook new actions to reduce tax evasion, especially VAT, and raise additional revenue through voluntary tax compliance.

- India implemented the Goods and Services Tax.
- Norway reduced its corporate tax rates from 25% to 24% and a further reduction to 23% is planned for 2018.
- Latvia replaced car and motorcycle taxes by an annual vehicle tax where rates are linked to CO_2 emission performance standards.
- Poland improved its VAT compliance, reflecting changes in the VAT Act and the Criminal Fiscal Code.
- Portugal reduced the preferential tax treatment of debt relative to equity, notably with the introduction of a tax allowance for corporate equity.
- Spain took several measures to broaden the corporate income tax base. Taxes on alcohol and tobacco have been increased. Furthermore, an electronic VAT filing system to address VAT fraud has been legislated.
- Switzerland increased the CO_2 levy from CHF 84 to CHF 96.
- The United States has cut the corporate tax rate from 35% to 21%.

Table 1.6. Recommendations and actions on the structure and efficiency of the tax system

	Broaden the tax base/reduce tax expenditures	Shift tax burden to property	Shift tax burden to environment	Shift tax burden to VAT	Improve tax collection/ compliance	Reduce corporate tax rate	Reduce the scope of VAT reduced rates	Reduce top income tax rates
Australia								
Austria								
Belgium								
Canada								
Czech Republic								
Denmark								
Estonia								
EU								
Finland								
France								
Germany								
Greece								
Hungary								
Iceland								
Ireland								
Israel								
Italy								
Japan								
Korea								
Latvia								
Lithuania								
Luxembourg								
Netherlands								
Norway								
New Zealand								
Poland								
Portugal								
Slovak Republic								
Slovenia								
Spain								
Sweden								
Switzerland								
United Kingdom								
United States								
Argentina								
Brazil								
Chile								
China								
Colombia								
Costa Rica								
Indonesia								
India								
Mexico								
Russia								
South Africa								
Turkey								

Note: Blue cells represent recommendations for a given country in a given area (with no action taken in 2017). Maroon cells represent actions taken on a recommendation (fully implemented or in the process of implementation).

1.5.3. Reforms to improve physical and legal infrastructure

Public investment contributes both directly and indirectly to the economy-wide capital stock, including through its role as a catalyst for private investment. Indeed, recent empirical work suggests a large positive effect of public investment on productivity (Fournier, 2016). As a result, enhancing the capacity and regulation of infrastructure is a priority in several advanced countries (Table 1.7). The emphasis is on addressing infrastructure shortages in a cost-effective way, in the area of transport, energy or both. Infrastructure provision - quantity and quality - is also very poor in many emerging economies, and raising public investment should be accompanied by reforms of the regulatory environment to attract private investment and optimise use. Removing infrastructure bottlenecks in these countries, such as those in transport, can contribute to higher employment by facilitating the matching of workers and jobs, and to improved business dynamism as quality infrastructure is crucial to the mobility of goods and people. It can improve inclusiveness and well-being, e.g. by providing access to reliable energy, clean water and sanitation in emerging economies or efficient and accessible public transport more generally. While in some cases infrastructure expansion may face trade-offs with the environment (e.g. expansion of road infrastructure), in others it may actually improve environmental outcomes (e.g. public transport). Recent actions in this area include:

- Argentina developed new public-private partnerships (PPPs) in the energy sector and for the construction of an airport terminal.
- Greece introduced more competition in the electricity production market; the incumbent's market share is expected to fall from over 90% to 50%.
- India has increased electrification, especially in rural areas. Full coverage is planned for 2018.
- Indonesia increased its spending on infrastructure significantly. The government also injected more funds into the State Asset Management Agency (LMAN) for land acquisition to facilitate strategic projects, including roads, ports and dams. Electrification in rural areas has also been increased.
- Latvia carried out improvements of public roads using EU funds.
- The United Kingdom introduced the National Productivity Investment Fund (NPIF) in order to support investment in a number of productivity-enhancing areas, in particular transport and digital infrastructure. Notably, the NPIF will fund the government's new 5G strategy and local full-fibre broadband projects.

Table 1.7. Recommendations and actions in public infrastructure

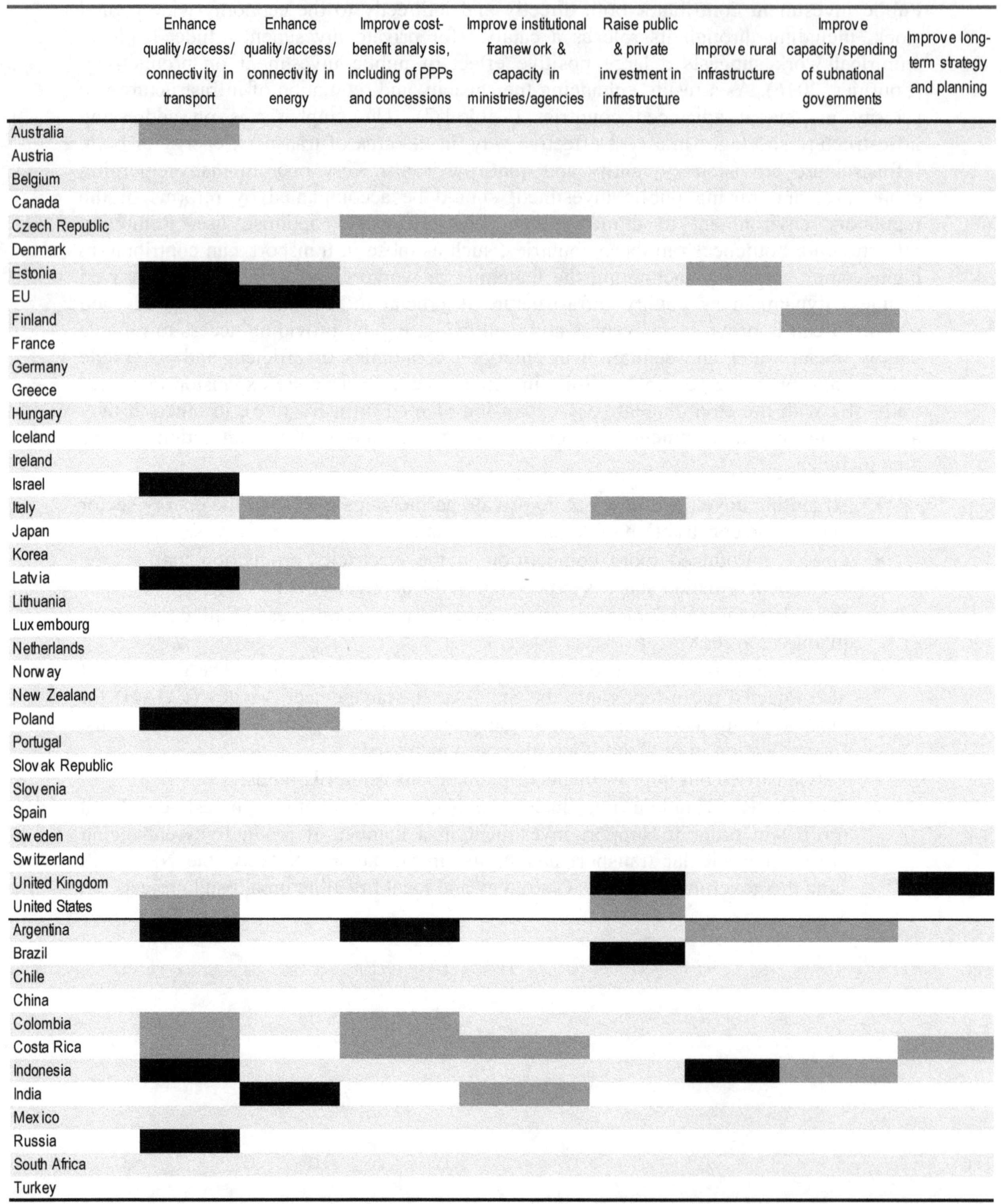

	Enhance quality/access/ connectivity in transport	Enhance quality/access/ connectivity in energy	Improve cost-benefit analysis, including of PPPs and concessions	Improve institutional framework & capacity in ministries/agencies	Raise public & private investment in infrastructure	Improve rural infrastructure	Improve capacity/spending of subnational governments	Improve long-term strategy and planning
Australia								
Austria								
Belgium								
Canada								
Czech Republic								
Denmark								
Estonia								
EU								
Finland								
France								
Germany								
Greece								
Hungary								
Iceland								
Ireland								
Israel								
Italy								
Japan								
Korea								
Latvia								
Lithuania								
Luxembourg								
Netherlands								
Norway								
New Zealand								
Poland								
Portugal								
Slovak Republic								
Slovenia								
Spain								
Sweden								
Switzerland								
United Kingdom								
United States								
Argentina								
Brazil								
Chile								
China								
Colombia								
Costa Rica								
Indonesia								
India								
Mexico								
Russia								
South Africa								
Turkey								

Note: Blue cells represent recommendations for a given country in a given area (with no action taken in 2017). Maroon cells represent actions taken on a recommendation (fully implemented or in the process of implementation).

Table 1.8. Recommendations and actions in rule of law and efficiency of public administration

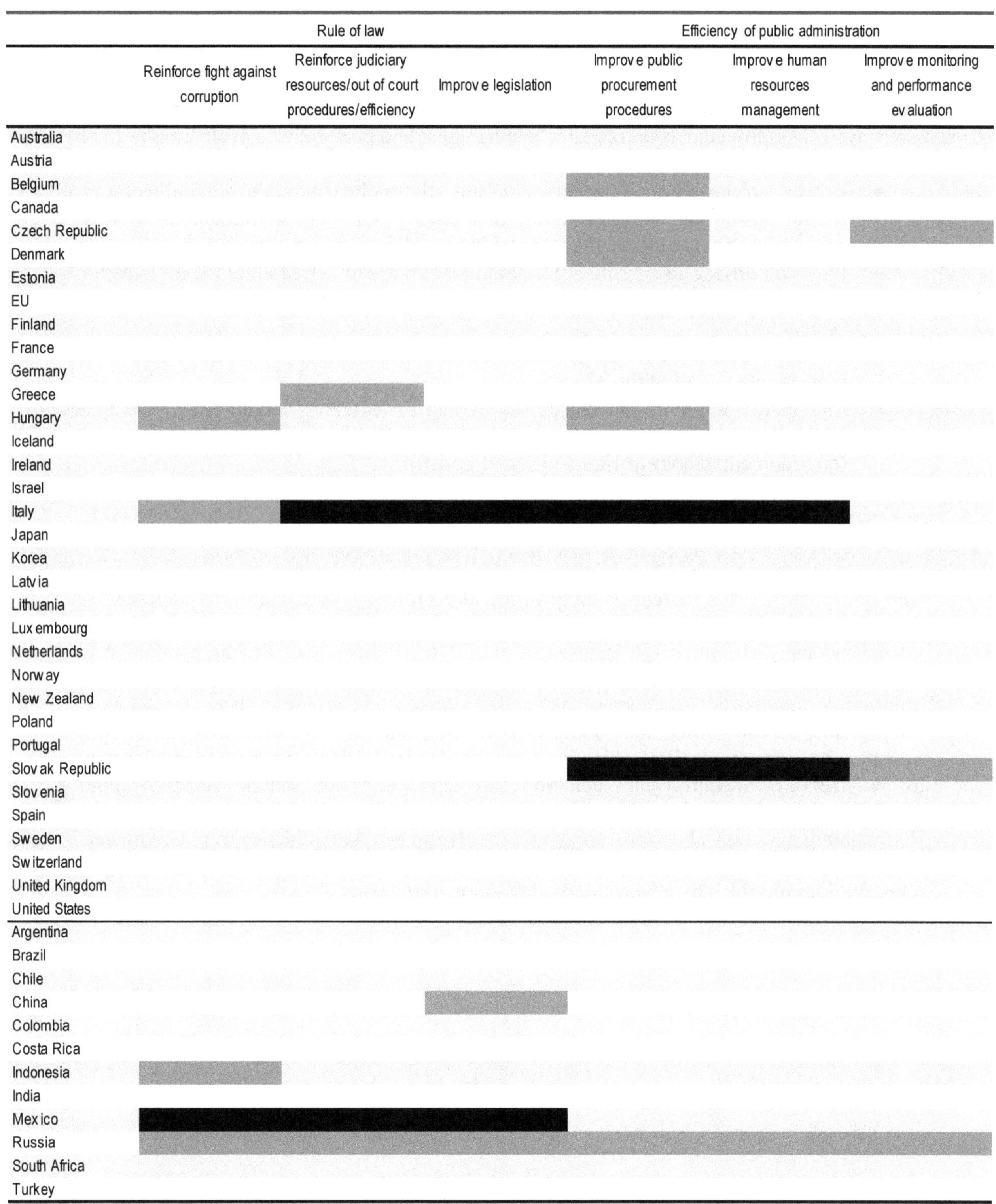

	Rule of law			Efficiency of public administration		
	Reinforce fight against corruption	Reinforce judiciary resources/out of court procedures/efficiency	Improve legislation	Improve public procurement procedures	Improve human resources management	Improve monitoring and performance evaluation
Australia						
Austria						
Belgium						
Canada						
Czech Republic						
Denmark						
Estonia						
EU						
Finland						
France						
Germany						
Greece						
Hungary						
Iceland						
Ireland						
Israel						
Italy						
Japan						
Korea						
Latvia						
Lithuania						
Luxembourg						
Netherlands						
Norway						
New Zealand						
Poland						
Portugal						
Slovak Republic						
Slovenia						
Spain						
Sweden						
Switzerland						
United Kingdom						
United States						
Argentina						
Brazil						
Chile						
China						
Colombia						
Costa Rica						
Indonesia						
India						
Mexico						
Russia						
South Africa						
Turkey						

Note: Blue cells represent recommendations for a given country in a given area (with no action taken in 2017). Maroon cells represent actions taken on a recommendation (fully implemented or in the process of implementation).

In addition to well-developed physical and digital infrastructure, a sound legal framework is also critical to lifting growth bottlenecks. Strengthening the overall institutional framework is important so that i) decisions defining policy needs are not skewed towards inefficient and unnecessary projects; ii) access to public services and justice is equally granted to all citizens; and iii) the main criteria to award contracts when procuring goods and services is value for money (Glaeser et al., 2004). *Going for Growth* provides policy options to strengthen the rule of law and judicial efficiency, with recommendations generally spanning the provision of security of persons and of property, the enforcement of contracts and checks on corruption as well as improvements on resource management and performance evaluation in public administrations. Recent actions in this area include (Table 1.8):

- Greece progressed on implementing the comprehensive public administration reform passed in 2016 and aiming at reducing political interference, as well as enhancing transparency and accountability, and fighting corruption.
- Italy modified its public procurement code to streamline and expedite implementations, based on the suggestions provided by the State Council and stakeholders.
- In Mexico, the New Anti-Corruption System has been approved and started to be implemented in all of the 32 states.
- The Slovak Republic introduced the "Value for Money" initiative, adopted in 3 sectors in 2016 (health, transports and ITC), and now expanded in 3 new sectors (environment, labour market and social policy).

1.6. Preserving social cohesion and helping workers make the most out of a dynamic labour market

Job-rich growth helps to reduce inequalities and promote more inclusive societies, as growth through labour utilisation gains tends to benefit disproportionately the lower-end of the income distribution (Hermansen et al., 2016). Policies that can be conducive to growth and inclusiveness jointly include those aimed at facilitating the participation and improving job-market outcomes of under-represented groups, such as women, immigrants, the low-skilled, the young, older workers and the disabled. *Going for Growth* recommendations target these objectives, notably by promoting a well-integrated system of passive (e.g. unemployment benefits) and active (e.g. job search support) labour market policies. These objectives also constitute some of the key pillars around which the forthcoming new *OECD Jobs Strategy* will revolve to provide guidance to policy makers on labour market and other policies that enable workers and firms to harness the opportunities provided by new technologies and markets (Box 1.1).

Box 1.1. The OECD's new Jobs Strategy

The OECD's new Jobs Strategy responds to global challenges related to the aftermath of the financial and economic crisis, continued weak productivity growth, high levels of income inequality in many countries, and the megatrends such as technological progress, globalisation, and ageing.

Strong and sustained economic growth remains a prerequisite for the quantity of jobs, but job quality, in terms of both wage and non-wage working conditions, and labour market inclusiveness, also emerges as a central policy priority. Policies to support flexibility in product and labour markets are needed for growth, but are not sufficient. Countries with policies and institutions that promote job quality, job quantity and greater inclusiveness perform better than countries where the focus is predominantly on market flexibility.

A whole-of-government response is needed, embedding the new OECD Jobs Strategy in the OECD Inclusive Growth Initiative as well as Going for Growth. The key policy recommendations are organised around three broad principles:

- ***Promoting an environment in which high-quality jobs can flourish.*** This requires a sound macroeconomic framework, a growth-friendly environment and skills evolving in line with market needs. A key new insight is that during sharp economic downturns it can be beneficial to channel resources to short-term work programmes that seek to preserve vulnerable jobs that are viable in the long-term. Moreover, the liberalisation of the use of temporary contracts while maintaining high levels of employment protection for workers on open-ended contracts can lead to the excessive use of temporary contracts and low job quality, high levels of inequality and low resilience, without clear gains in overall employment.
- ***Preventing labour market exclusion and protecting individuals against labour market risks.*** Protecting workers who fall through the cracks remains essential but it is important to address problems before they arise: strengthening the equality of opportunities and a life-course perspective to avoid an accumulation of individual disadvantages. New evidence suggests that a high coverage of the unemployment benefit and social assistance system, with rigorous enforcement of mutual obligations, plays a pivotal role in the success of activation strategies, providing a key instrument for connecting with the jobless.

Preparing for future opportunities and challenges in a rapidly changing economy and labour market. Product and labour market dynamism will be necessary to deal with rapid economic change. However, workers need to be equipped with the right skills in a context where the demand for skills is likely to evolve rapidly, potentially eroding incentives for investing in non-transferable skills. Workers also need to remain protected against labour market risks in a world where flexible forms of work may increase. This includes social protection and basic labour market regulations but possibly also expanding the role of non-contributory schemes, minimum floors to social benefits, and making social protection more portable. A more radical solution - a universal basic income (UBI) - is unlikely to provide effective protection to all workers without significantly raising fiscal pressure or the need to cut other, well-targeted benefits to finance the UBI.

Matching efficiency, i.e. the ease with which jobseekers find jobs according to their skills has deteriorated in recent years (European Commission, 2014), reflecting the growing mismatch in terms of skills, industries and regions. Reforms that ease labour market restrictions and promote worker mobility, e.g. property transaction costs, rental regulation, can reduce the number of unfilled job vacancies, and boost productivity and inclusiveness by facilitating a better matching of worker's skills and jobs tasks.

Finally, health is a key ingredient of well-being overall, and promoting better health provides people with higher life satisfaction and a platform to fulfil their productive potential. People in ill-health are less able to take part in productive activities, but people working in poor labour conditions are also more likely to find themselves afflicted by illness. Recent OECD evidence shows that income, lifestyle choices and the environment are all significantly associated with gains in life expectancy (James et al 2015), while healthier people tend to benefit from greater access to training opportunities, and can expect their children to attain stronger educational results.

1.6.1. Reforms to reduce the gender gap in labour market participation and work conditions

A high proportion of women remain outside of, or poorly attached to, the labour market in a number of countries, while in others they are overrepresented among (involuntary) part-time workers (OECD, 2016c). Recommendations are made to encourage female labour force participation or hours worked where those are particularly low and can be traced to ill-designed existing policies. Hence, recommendations include family-friendly policies and working conditions which enable fathers and mothers to balance their working hours and their family responsibilities and facilitate women's employment. They fall in three main reform areas – with differential thrust reflecting country-specific context (Table 1.9): i) the level and design of taxes and benefits and systems of joint taxation (e.g. tax allowances for non-working spouses), ii) high costs, weak targeting and therefore limited access to childcare, and iii) ill-designed parental leave policies with low de facto take-up of parental leave arising from, for example, the lack of flexibility in working-time arrangements and underdeveloped part-time work. Addressing these challenges would allow for a better balance between work and family and a narrowing of gender inequalities, bringing equity and welfare gains. Recent actions in this area include:

- The newly adopted "Education Investment Law" in Austria will provide EUR 750 million for the expansion of full-day schooling until 2025.
- Germany boosted funding for child day care services by approximately EUR 1.1 billion, from 2017 to 2020.
- Japan is implementing a significant new plan to gradually expand the capacity of childcare centres by 320 thousand children by 2020. Teleworking rules have been also revised to allow more flexibility in teleworking and flexitime systems.
- Korea raised the amount of parental leave benefits for the first three months of leave.
- Luxembourg introduced optional individual taxation for both resident and cross-border married or co-habiting workers in order to reduce the marginal tax rate applied to the earnings of second earners.

Table 1.9. Recommendations and actions for stronger labour market participation of women and the integration of migrants and minorities

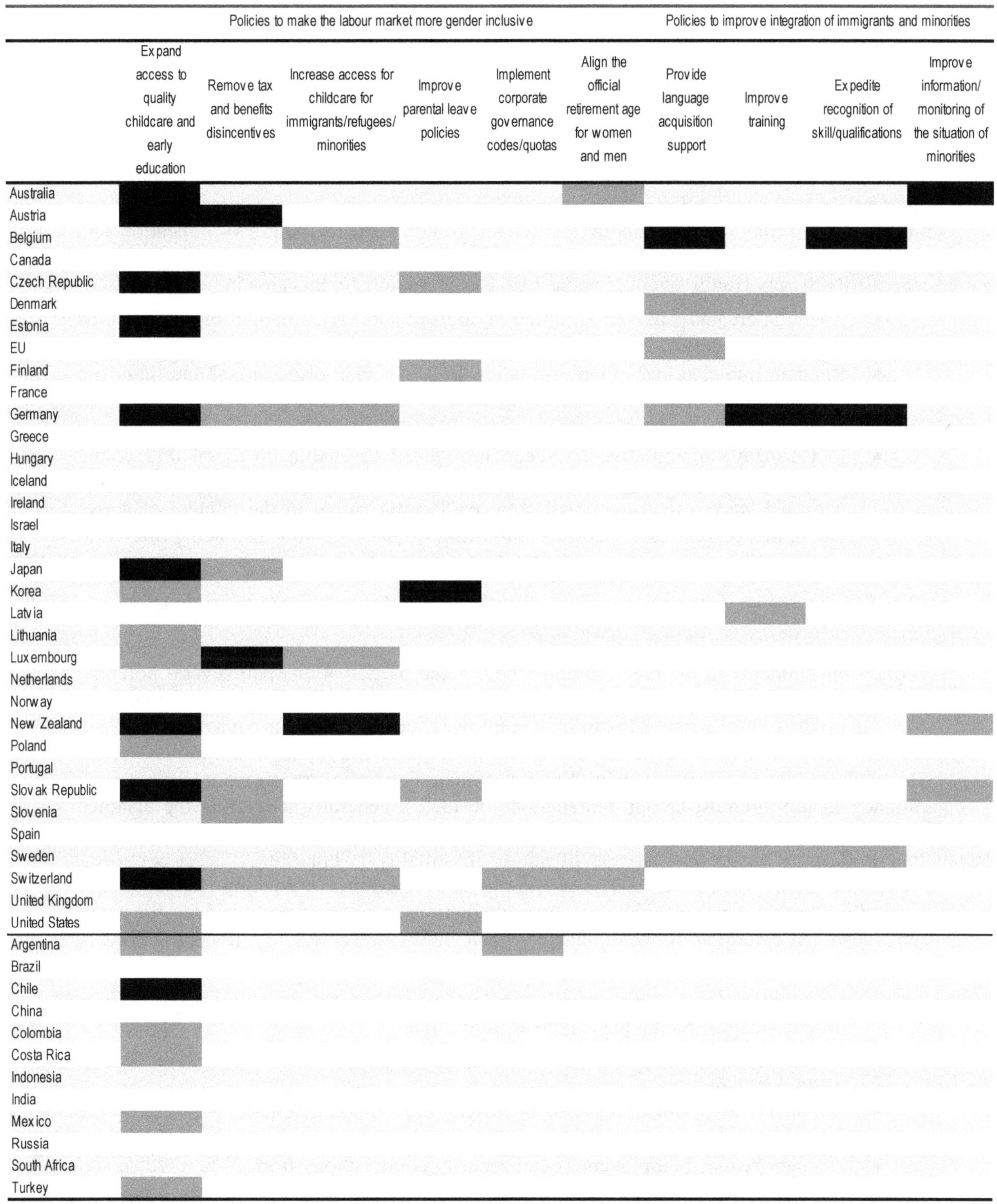

	Policies to make the labour market more gender inclusive						Policies to improve integration of immigrants and minorities			
	Expand access to quality childcare and early education	Remove tax and benefits disincentives	Increase access for childcare for immigrants/refugees/ minorities	Improve parental leave policies	Implement corporate governance codes/quotas	Align the official retirement age for women and men	Provide language acquisition support	Improve training	Expedite recognition of skill/qualifications	Improve information/ monitoring of the situation of minorities
Australia										
Austria										
Belgium										
Canada										
Czech Republic										
Denmark										
Estonia										
EU										
Finland										
France										
Germany										
Greece										
Hungary										
Iceland										
Ireland										
Israel										
Italy										
Japan										
Korea										
Latvia										
Lithuania										
Luxembourg										
Netherlands										
Norway										
New Zealand										
Poland										
Portugal										
Slovak Republic										
Slovenia										
Spain										
Sweden										
Switzerland										
United Kingdom										
United States										
Argentina										
Brazil										
Chile										
China										
Colombia										
Costa Rica										
Indonesia										
India										
Mexico										
Russia										
South Africa										
Turkey										

Note: Blue cells represent recommendations for a given country in a given area (with no action taken in 2017). Maroon cells represent actions taken on a recommendation (fully implemented or in the process of implementation).

1.6.2. Reforms to integrate migrants and minorities

The share of the foreign-born population has increased significantly across advanced countries, reaching now nearly 10% of the total population. Second-generation immigrants are also numerous and heterogeneous, and several advanced countries have sizeable minorities, such as Roma or aboriginal populations. At the same time, refugee flows have recently increased significantly, especially to European countries. This increasing population diversity can bring significant economic and social benefits to OECD countries, such as easing demographic pressure on labour participation. But the realisation of these benefits will depend largely on the design and implementation of integration measures. *Going for Growth* recommendations in this area range from measures to promote rapid labour market integration to early action in education and social domains that could facilitate labour market integration in the future and reduce inequality of opportunity overall (Table 1.9). Recent actions in this area include:

- Australia created a new programme (Youth Jobs PaTH) aimed at improving skills and opportunities of indigenous communities
- Belgium included in its Plan Formation 2020 a social, professional and linguistic assessment of migrants as well as specific offers of training and/or validation for newly arrived migrants.
- In Germany, an initiative has been introduced to enable up to 10 000 young refugees to start training in the skilled crafts sector. Moreover, refugees can now get quick access to some small-scale paid employment in the context of active labour market policies. Specific counselling services are now also being offered to young immigrants.

1.6.3. Reforms to reduce obstacles to job creation, labour force participation and employment in formal sector jobs

Policy impediments to job creation and labour force participation span several potential areas of actions. First, high labour tax wedges can reduce firms' labour demand by driving up the cost of labour (due to high employers' contributions or payroll taxes). As a result, high labour tax wedges are associated with lower employment and hours worked as well as higher unemployment. Such detrimental effects are stronger for workers already facing foremost labour demand-side obstacles, generally the youth, the disabled and the low-skilled, and the elderly. Too high, ill-designed social security provisions and tax wedges are also major drivers of labour informality in emerging-market countries, reflecting both labour demand and supply-side obstacles. Reducing labour taxes, including through cuts in social security contributions, thus remains a priority for many advanced and emerging-market countries (Table 1.10 and Table 1.11). Recent actions in this area include:

- In addition to the tax reform that entered into force in 2016, Austria is progressively reducing payroll taxes until 2018.
- Estonia introduced continuous training measures targeted to those at risk of unemployment.
- In Finland, fiscal measures associated with the Competitiveness Pact reduced the tax wedge.
- Hungary reduced employers' social security contributions from 27% to 22%, and will reduce them by a further 2 percentage points in 2018.
- Turkey reduced employers' social security contributions from 14% to 9% of gross wages. Moreover, for firms that have increased their net employment over 2016, new hiring will be exempt of social security contributions for one year.

Table 1.10. Recommendations and actions to lift obstacles to labour force participation and employment

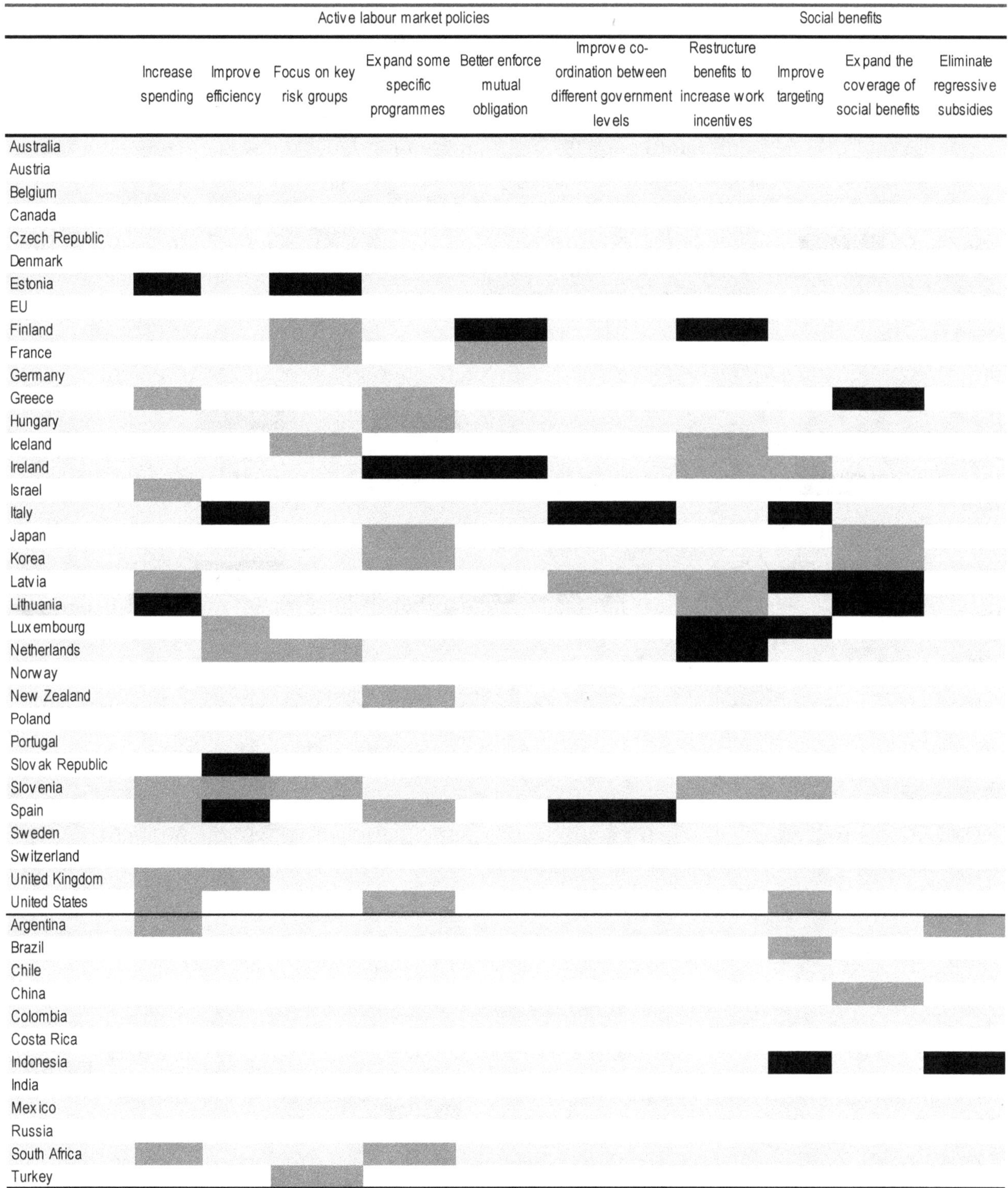

	Active labour market policies						Social benefits			
	Increase spending	Improve efficiency	Focus on key risk groups	Expand some specific programmes	Better enforce mutual obligation	Improve co-ordination between different government levels	Restructure benefits to increase work incentives	Improve targeting	Expand the coverage of social benefits	Eliminate regressive subsidies
Australia										
Austria										
Belgium										
Canada										
Czech Republic										
Denmark										
Estonia										
EU										
Finland										
France										
Germany										
Greece										
Hungary										
Iceland										
Ireland										
Israel										
Italy										
Japan										
Korea										
Latvia										
Lithuania										
Luxembourg										
Netherlands										
Norway										
New Zealand										
Poland										
Portugal										
Slovak Republic										
Slovenia										
Spain										
Sweden										
Switzerland										
United Kingdom										
United States										
Argentina										
Brazil										
Chile										
China										
Colombia										
Costa Rica										
Indonesia										
India										
Mexico										
Russia										
South Africa										
Turkey										

Note: Blue cells represent recommendations for a given country in a given area (with no action taken in 2017). Maroon cells represent actions taken on a recommendation (fully implemented or in the process of implementation).

Table 1.11. Recommendations and actions to lift obstacles to labour force participation and employment

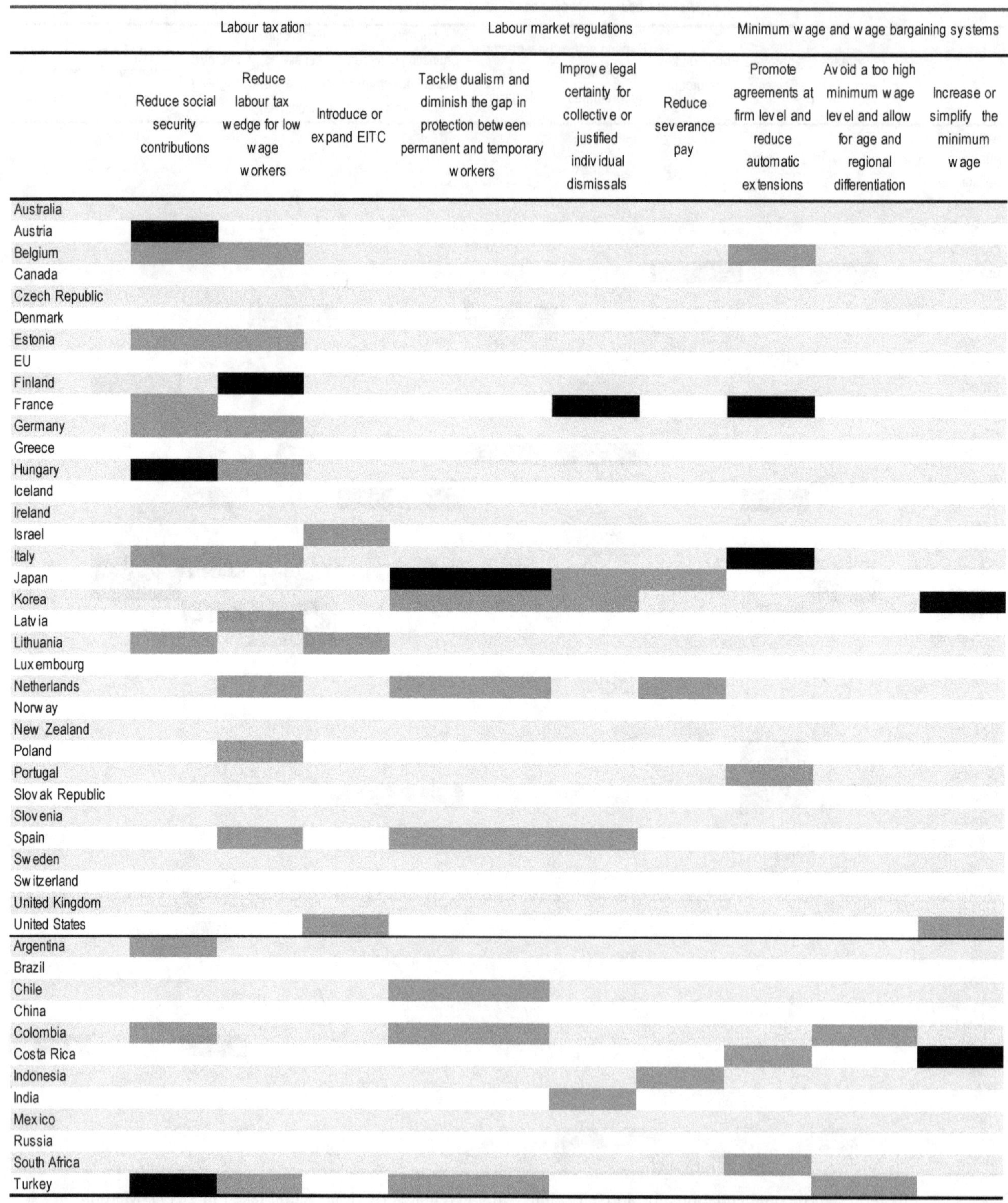

	Labour taxation			Labour market regulations			Minimum wage and wage bargaining systems		
	Reduce social security contributions	Reduce labour tax wedge for low wage workers	Introduce or expand EITC	Tackle dualism and diminish the gap in protection between permanent and temporary workers	Improve legal certainty for collective or justified individual dismissals	Reduce severance pay	Promote agreements at firm level and reduce automatic extensions	Avoid a too high minimum wage level and allow for age and regional differentiation	Increase or simplify the minimum wage
Australia									
Austria									
Belgium									
Canada									
Czech Republic									
Denmark									
Estonia									
EU									
Finland									
France									
Germany									
Greece									
Hungary									
Iceland									
Ireland									
Israel									
Italy									
Japan									
Korea									
Latvia									
Lithuania									
Luxembourg									
Netherlands									
Norway									
New Zealand									
Poland									
Portugal									
Slovak Republic									
Slovenia									
Spain									
Sweden									
Switzerland									
United Kingdom									
United States									
Argentina									
Brazil									
Chile									
China									
Colombia									
Costa Rica									
Indonesia									
India									
Mexico									
Russia									
South Africa									
Turkey									

Note: Blue cells represent recommendations for a given country in a given area (with no action taken in 2017). Maroon cells represent actions taken on a recommendation (fully implemented or in the process of implementation).

Second, the articulation between unemployment benefits, social protection and active labour market policies should be designed to provide adequate income support during jobless spells while encouraging the return to work, efficiently matching workers and jobs. The challenge consists in designing social protection systems that minimise trade-offs between financial sustainability, adequacy and efficiency (Fall et al., 2015). At the same time, a large number of countries still need to address long-term unemployment and bring those discouraged by long unemployment spells back into the labour market. This requires targeted policies, such as a more intensive and personalised approach to case management (e.g. regular face-to-face interviews and the development of individual action plans) as well as measures to find job opportunities that contribute to skills acquisition and work experience. The importance of ALMPs is now well established, as reflected in the sustained pace of reforms in this area since the post-crisis period. But despite this encouraging progress, reforms in this area are still needed, with differential emphasis depending on country-specific performance and policy challenges (Table 1.10). Recent actions in this area include:

- Finland tightened job-search reporting requirements and reduced the duration of unemployment insurance.
- Greece rolled out nation-wide its "Social Solidarity Income" (SSI), with supporting infrastructure for identifying eligible households and transferring funds.
- Italy implemented a nationwide anti-poverty programme, with the creation of the 'Inclusive Income' scheme to tackle severe poverty especially among families with children.
- Lithuania enacted the Law on Employment, which changes the structure of public employment services, centralising the management of activities planning, financial and human resources. The law also strengthens activation policies by scrutinising active labour market measures, extending the scope of employment support and widening training possibilities for the unemployed.
- Luxembourg strengthened eligibility conditions for unemployment benefit recipients and included the requirement to actively search for employment and retrain.
- The Slovak Republic amended its previous Act on Employment Services to improve the access of jobseekers to training and to widen the range of available measures.

Third, too stringent labour market regulations and collective bargaining systems slow down the reallocation process and thus aggregate productivity growth because they raise labour adjustment costs for firms (Haltiwanger et al., 2006). A clear tendency towards reducing the strictness of employment protection has been observed over the past decade, mostly focussed on regulations governing individual and collective dismissals. In the aftermath of the crisis, more than one-third of advanced economies undertook some relaxation of these regulations, with reforms concentrated in countries with the most stringent provisions. However, most of the easing took place for non-regular contracts, leading to their expansion and a heightened duality on the labour market. High labour market duality can have adverse impacts on both equity and efficiency, as the young tend to be confined in these contracts between unemployment spells and thus suffer from skill depreciation, which translates in lower productivity over all.

Reforms in this area are thus still needed in a number of countries (Table 1.11). The emphasis is on simplifying procedures and reducing costs and uncertainties associated with lay-offs but at the same time strengthening the protection of individuals (as opposed to jobs). This requires having in place adequate income support for the unemployed as well as effective job-search counselling and re-employment services (see above). As a result, job protection recommendations are often formulated as part of broader labour market reform packages, with differential emphasis depending on countries' challenges and weaknesses. Recent actions in this area include:

- In Japan, the guidelines for equal pay for equal work have been set out to improve the treatment of non-regular workers and to help them receive judicial relief in the case of discrimination. The government will submit the relevant bills to the Diet.
- As part of its major labour market reform, France streamlined workers' representation and sector-specific agreements will have to include specific conditions for small and medium enterprises. The Labour Minister and individual firms now have more leeway to base administrative extensions on an evaluation of their economic and social effects. In the case of employment protection legislation, a ceiling on the compensation paid by the employer in the case of unfair dismissal has been introduced, reducing legal uncertainties.

Finally, low-paid employment is a policy concern when it is associated with in-work poverty or reflects situations where workers are unable to get wages in line with their productivity or to find jobs that make full use of their skills. In particular, setting the level of the minimum wage requires a careful balancing. Too low net minimum wages can fail to assure adequate living standards and are likely to be ineffective in fostering incentives to work for individuals at the margin of the labour market, while a minimum wage set too high can reduce firms' incentives to hire or to formalise employment of low-skilled workers. Policies and institutions can help to set minimum wages appropriately and minimise any adverse employment effects. Reforms in this area are recommended for countries where ill-designed minimum wage policies appear to weigh on low-skilled or formal employment (Table 1.11). Recent actions in this area include:

- Korea increased the minimum wage by 7.3%, to 56% of the median wage, a ratio that is close to the OECD average.

1.6.4. Reforms to reduce policy barriers to mobility

Institutional settings regulating (residential and commercial) property and land-use can discourage labour as well as capital mobility, often by distorting the price responsiveness of rental and construction supply and demand conditions. Country-specific recommendations in this area are formulated with a view to boost both labour utilisation and labour productivity (Table 1.12). This policy area can nonetheless raise trade-offs with equity. One example is social housing, which is an important tool to improve access to affordable housing among vulnerable households, but may act as a barrier to labour mobility. Recent actions in this area include:

- Denmark modernised land use regulation, notably to allow larger retail stores and better opportunities for tourism in rural areas.
- In the United Kingdom, the Housing Infrastructure Fund was introduced to unlock land from local councils in order to deliver 100 000 new homes in areas of high demand with a total investment of GBP 5 billion. Additionally, GBP 2 billion will be dedicated to the funding of affordable housing, including funding for homes let at a social rent.

Table 1.12. Recommendations and actions to address workers' mobility and health sector efficiency

	Housing policies					Health sector efficiency		
	Ease planning and construction regulations	Reduce/eliminate preferential tax treatments	Reduce rent regulation	Improve targeting of social housing/subsidies	Increase the supply of social housing	Promote and improve generics drugs use	Reinforce/monitor equity in access	Promote more healthy lifestyles
Australia								
Austria								
Belgium								
Canada								
Czech Republic								
Denmark								
Estonia								
EU								
Finland								
France								
Germany								
Greece								
Hungary								
Iceland								
Ireland								
Israel								
Italy								
Japan								
Korea								
Latvia								
Lithuania								
Luxembourg								
Netherlands								
Norway								
New Zealand								
Poland								
Portugal								
Slovak Republic								
Slovenia								
Spain								
Sweden								
Switzerland								
United Kingdom								
United States								
Argentina								
Brazil								
Chile								
China								
Colombia								
Costa Rica								
Indonesia								
India								
Mexico								
Russia								
South Africa								
Turkey								

Note: Blue cells represent recommendations for a given country in a given area (with no action taken in 2017). Maroon cells represent actions taken on a recommendation (fully implemented or in the process of implementation).

1.6.5. Reforms to address public healthcare challenges

Addressing the determinants of population health and health inequalities requires policies across multiple sectors for achieving better social, education and labour market outcomes and thereby more inclusive growth and well-being. Among them, reforms to promote health sector efficiency and healthy lifestyles feature regularly among *Going for Growth* recommendations, and in some countries the scope for improvement remains large (Table 1.12). Recent actions in this area include:

- China linked 361 regions (96% of the total) and 8624 cross-regional medical institutions to the nationwide settlement system for medical expenses. This will improve the utilisation of health services by migrant workers and reduce the time between when health costs are incurred and reimbursed.
- Lithuania increased excise duties on alcohol and tobacco products to promote healthy lifestyles. The number of municipal public health bureaus, responsible for health promotion and disease prevention, has also been increased.
- Switzerland adopted a decree which aims at decreasing generic drugs prices by comparing them with international prices and by linking the price with the turnover made by the original maker.

Endnotes

1. In this publication, the group of advanced economies comprises all OECD member countries excluding Chile, Mexico and Turkey but includes Lithuania. Chile, Mexico and Turkey have been considered as part of the group of emerging economies alongside Argentina, Brazil, China, Colombia, Costa Rica, Indonesia, India, Russia and South Africa.

2. No past information on the importance of the reforms taken exists.

References

Andrews, D. and F. Cingano (2012), "Public policy and resource allocation: Evidence from firms in OECD countries", OECD Economics Department Working Papers No. 996, OECD Publishing, Paris.

Andrews, D., C. Criscuolo and P. Gal (2015), "Frontier firms, technology diffusion and public policy: Micro Evidence from OECD Countries", OECD Productivity Working Papers No. 2, OECD Publishing, Paris.

Andrews, D., C. Criscuolo and Peter N. Gal (2016), "The Best versus the rest: The global productivity slowdown, divergence across firms and the role of public policy," OECD Productivity Working Papers No. 5, OECD Publishing, Paris.

Arnold, J., B. Brys, C. Heady, A. Johansson, C. Schwellnus, and L. Vartia (2011), "Tax Policy for Economic Recovery and Growth", The Economic Journal, Vol. 121, Royal Economic Society.

Causa, O., M. Hermansen and N. Ruiz (2016), "The distributional impact of structural reforms", OECD Economics Department Working Papers No. 1342, OECD Publishing, Paris.

Calvino, F. and M. E. Virgillito (2016), "The Innovation-Employment nexus: a critical survey of theory and empirics", LEM Papers Series 2016/10, Laboratory of Economics and Management (LEM), Sant'Anna School of Advanced Studies, Pisa, Italy.

Égert, B. and P. Gal (2017), "The Quantification of Structural Reforms in OECD Countries: A new Framework," OECD Economics Department Working Papers No. 1354, OECD Publishing, Paris.

European Commission (2014), "Is unemployment structural or cyclical? Main features of job matching in the EU after the crisis", Economic Papers No. 527, European Commission.

Fall, F., D. Bloch, J-M Fournier, and P. Hoeller (2015), "Prudent debt targets and fiscal frameworks," OECD Economic Policy Papers No. 15, OECD Publishing, Paris.

Fournier, J-M. (2016), "The positive effect of public investment on potential growth", OECD Economics Department Working Papers No. 1347, OECD Publishing, Paris.

Glaeser, E., R. LaPorta, R.F. Lopez-de-Silanes and A. Shleifer (2004), "Do institutions cause growth?", Journal of Economic Growth, Vol. 9, Elsevier.

Haltiwanger, J., S. Scarpetta and H. Schweiger (2006), "Assessing job flows across countries: The role of industry, firm size and regulations", IZA Discussion Paper No. 2450, Bonn.

Heckman, J., L. Lochner and P. Todd (2005), "Earning functions, rates of return, and treatment effects: The Mincer equation and beyond", NBER Working Paper, No. 11544, National Bureau of Economic Research.

Hermansen, M., N. Ruiz and O. Causa (2016), "The distribution of the growth dividends", OECD Economics Department Working Papers, No. 1343, OECD Publishing, Paris.

James, C., M. Devaux, C. Marechal, and F. Sassi F (2015), "Inclusive growth and health", OECD Employment, Labour and Social Affairs Health Division Committee Paper.

OECD (2013), Interconnected Economies: Benefiting from Global Value Chains, OECD Publishing, Paris.

OECD (2015), The Future of Productivity, OECD Publishing, Paris.

OECD (2016a), Inequality Update – November 2016, OECD Publishing, Paris.

OECD (2016b), The Productivity-Inclusiveness Nexus, OECD Publishing, Paris.

OECD (2016c), OECD Employment Outlook 2016, OECD Publishing, Paris.

OECD (2017), Economic Policy Reforms 2017: Going for Growth, OECD Publishing, Paris.

Ollivaud, P., Y. Guillemette and D. Turner (2016), "Links between weak investment and the slowdown in productivity and potential output growth across the OECD", OECD Economics Department Working Papers, No. 1304, OECD Publishing, Paris.

Annex 1.A. Structural policy indicators

Starting from the 2018 issue of *Going for Growth*, the chapter on Structural Policy Indicators is now only available online, under the following address:

http://www.oecd.org/eco/growth/going-for-growth

This chapter contains a comprehensive set of quantitative indicators that allow for a comparison of policy settings across countries (both OECD and selected non-OECD depending on data availability). The indicators cover areas of tax and transfer systems and how they affect work incentives, as well as product and labour market regulations, education and training, trade and investment rules and innovation policies. The indicators are presented in the form of figures showing for all countries the most recent available observation and the change relative to the previous observation.

Chapter 2. Going for green(er) growth - what can indicators tell us?

This chapter reviews the available green growth indicators with respect to their usefulness for the potential integration in Going for Growth *in the future as well as broadly evaluates country scores and progress on them. The chapter also flags the key measurement gaps that will be crucial in determining the scope and depth of green growth coverage in* Going for Growth. *The Annex provides additional information on the main green growth indicators that would be potential inputs to the* Going for Growth *process.*

The statistical data for Israel are supplied by and under the responsibility of the relevant Israeli authorities. The use of such data by the OECD is without prejudice to the status of the Golan Heights, East Jerusalem and Israeli settlements in the West Bank under the terms of international law.

Main findings

- A clean and healthy environment is essential for supporting economic activity and well-being in the long-term. Practically every economic and leisure activity – as well as life itself - has broadly-defined environment as a key input and could not exist without it.
- Yet, the links between the environment and economic growth as such are complex and not very well documented.
- There exists no single broadly accepted measure of environmental performance that could be used for the *Going for Growth* exercise. However, significant progress has been made in measurement of green growth outcomes, challenges and policies, notably as part of the OECD Green Growth Indicators.
- The areas of best coverage of measurement of environmental outcomes include climate, air pollution and land use. Progress has also been made in the measurement of so-called green innovation.
- Indicators on waste, waste water treatment and water efficiency, as well as on water pollution and scarcity are less well developed, and unlikely to be suitable for systematic use in *Going for Growth* at this point. The measurement of risks also needs to be improved.
- Despite recent progress, the indicators of environmental policies are not yet well developed and of limited coverage. The ability to better measure policies is crucial for improving the empirical evidence on their impacts.
- The scope of future integration of Green Growth in *Going for Growth* will depend crucially on the progress in measurement and the empirical evidence on the links among various dimensions such as growth and well-being, the environment, and environmental policies.

Going for Growth targets long-term economic growth and well-being through the identification of structural reform priorities for OECD member and key non-member economies. The ability to sustain long-term improvements in GDP and well-being depends – among other things - on the ability to reduce negative effects (such as pollution) associated with economic activity, as well as to minimise environment-related risks and the reliance on (limited) natural capital resources as a source of growth. In this respect, the *Going for Growth* goals, described as "a policy agenda for growth to benefit all" are inherently intertwined with green growth (GG) – which adds an environmental sustainability dimension: "*fostering economic growth and development while ensuring that natural assets continue to provide the resources and environmental services on which our well-being relies.*" (OECD, 2011).

A combined assessment of economic, social and environmental progress and challenges underpins the effective implementation of Sustainable Development Goals. The 2017 issue of *Going for Growth* focussed on the integration of inclusiveness into the priority selection framework. One year later, the time has come for a first step in exploring the potential green growth angle of *Going for Growth* (OECD, 2017a). In this respect, measurement and indicators are a key foundation for better taking account of the environment and green growth policy reforms. This chapter reviews the available indicators with respect to their usefulness for the potential integration in *Going for Growth* in the future as well as broadly evaluates country scores and progress on them.[3] The chapter also flags the key measurement gaps that will be crucial in determining the scope and depth of green growth coverage in *Going for Growth.* The Annex provides additional information on the main GG indicators that would be potential inputs to the *Going for Growth* process.

2.1. Environment and growth (and well-being)

A clean and healthy environment is essential for supporting economic activity and well-being in the long-term. Practically every economic and leisure activity – as well as life itself - has broadly-defined environment as a key input and could not exist without it. However, the relationship between the environment and GDP growth per se is more complex. For example, looking at the contributions to GDP growth in OECD and large emerging market economies (Argentina, Brazil, Russia, India, Indonesia, China and South Africa) over the past two decades, the main source has been multifactor productivity growth, followed by capital deepening (Figure 2.1).

A framework developed at the OECD allows evaluating the sources of growth in a broader sense - adjusting growth outcomes for "bad" outputs air emissions (greenhouse gasses and air pollutants) and calculating the contribution of subsoil asset use – that is, distinguishing to what extent classically measured growth has been higher (lower) due to increased pollution or increased exploitation of natural subsoil assets.[4] Still, the adjustment for emissions is sizeably negative only for China, India, Korea, Costa Rica, Turkey and Mexico, indicating a significant part of growth in these countries was achieved at the expense of the environment. This adjustment is negligible for other countries, or even positive in countries where the pollution performance improved. In Russia, Chile, China, Israel, China and Australia a considerable share of GDP growth was owed to increased subsoil resource extraction. For most other countries, underground mineral resources did not play a driving role in GDP growth.

The relationship between the environment and growth is much more complex and multidimensional than can be captured by this environmentally-adjusted multifactor productivity (EAMFP) concept. The EAMFP is severely limited by the breadth of the environmental areas covered: a handful of key air pollutant emissions, carbon dioxide and a selection of extractable resources. Still, even if the environment may not have stood out as a key driver of macroeconomic growth in the past, it is essential for maintaining production and incomes, and some broad linking themes can be identified:

- *The sustainability of growth (and well-being).* Economic activity, consumption and lifestyles rely on exhaustible resources and limited capacity of the environment to absorb the unwanted by-products of production and consumption (so-called sink functions). Many of the key relationships are highly non-linear, the thresholds and bottlenecks are imprecise, location- and time-specific, or simply not well known. Still, surpassing certain levels of degradation will lead to high costs in terms of physical and psychological health damages, or by engaging productive resources in necessary clean-up, remediation or adaptation.
- *Environmentally-related risks to future growth paths.* Such risks have similar detrimental effects to growth and well-being as above, but are more a question of an increasing probability than affecting the central scenario. That is, environmental degradation can increase the risks related to large-scale, catastrophic events. A prime example is the increasing likelihood of extreme weather events associated with climate change.
- *Well-being aspects that are not necessarily linked to growth.* Many aspects of well-being, such as health, morbidity and premature mortality or the utility of access to environmental amenities are often difficult to quantify in terms of tangible costs or GDP.
- *Public goods and cross-border effects.* An additional complication is that damages and risks do not always fall on the country responsible for generating them, for example, as in the case of global externalities related to climate change or cross-border pollution. In this respect, the constraints may come from international commitments rather than actual domestic damages and risks.
- *Social inclusion and the distribution of effects.* Even if many environment-related developments and risks are limited on average (or at the macro level), they may have significant impacts on parts of the society (in particular those vulnerable), the local economy and specific sectors.

Tracking progress on greening growth effectively means tracking the sustainability of growth and well-being improvements, the contribution to meeting global environmental challenges and the ability to keep potential risks in check. Our ability to do so remains limited but has advanced sufficiently to allow a first step of the integration into *Going for Growth.*

Figure 2.1. The sources of growth: accounting for the environment[1]

Total economy, long-term average growth rates, circa 1991-2013

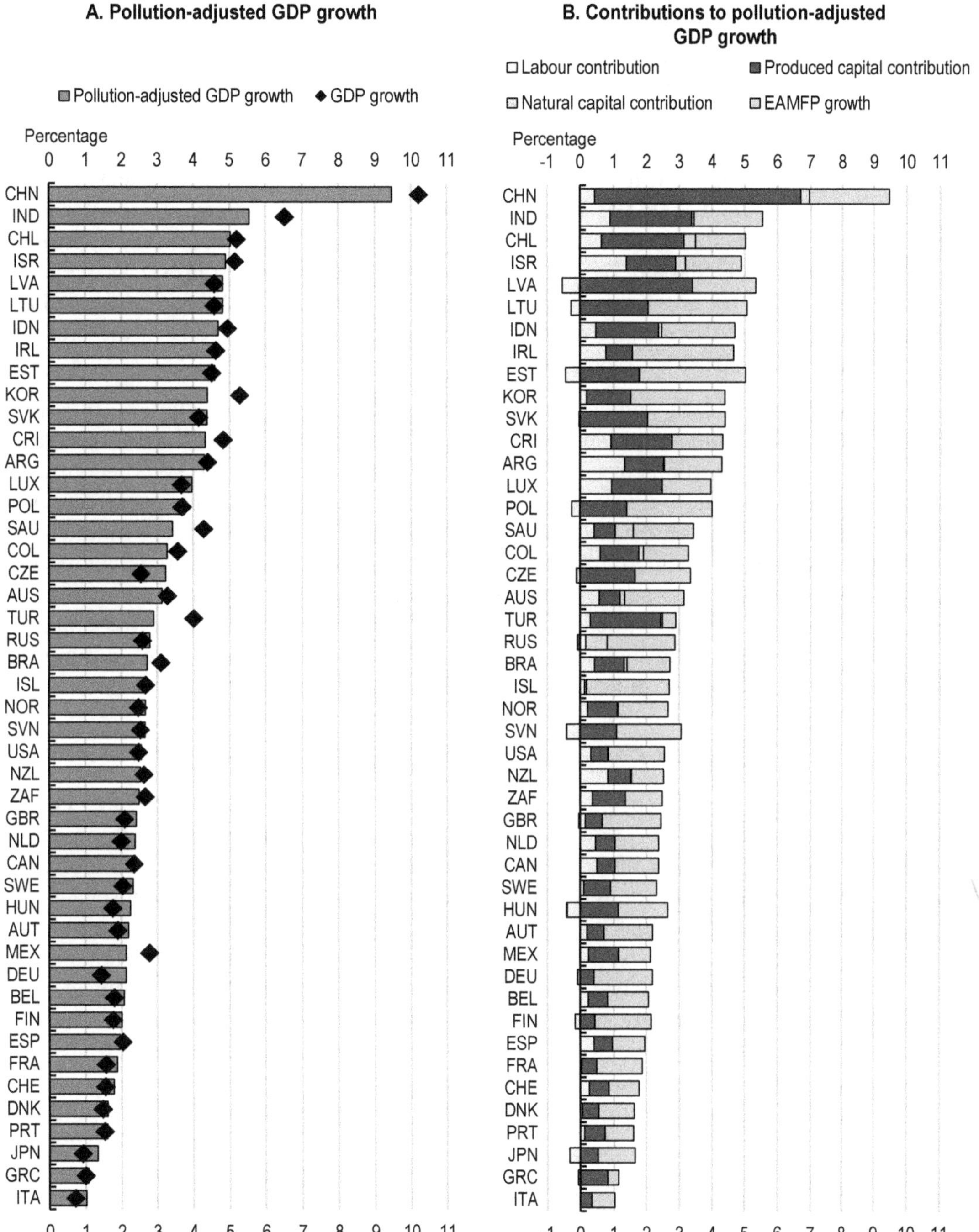

1. EAMFP stands for environmentally-adjusted multi factor productivity. The coverage of environmental services remains partial, currently limited to subsoil assets on the input side ("natural capital") and air emissions as undesirable output. In panel B, negative values mean that the contribution of natural capital (effectively subsoil asset extraction) to output growth has been decreasing.

Source: OECD (2017), Green Growth Indicators 2017.

StatLink http://dx.doi.org/10.1787/888933680210

2.2. Green growth – measuring performance and progress

There is no universal way of measuring performance and progress on green growth, primarily because of the elusiveness and multidimensionality of the green growth concept with respect to the available relevant indicators (Box 2.1). So-called green growth indicators – indicators measuring challenges and progress related to green growth – span a wide set of environmental, economic, social indicators as well as indicators that combine two or more of these dimensions. Such a set is potentially inexhaustible. In practice, it is only possible to synthesise the key dimensions of green growth, those where some consensus on their priority means data has been developed and collected. The OECD's Environment and Statistics Directorates have proposed a framework to approach the measurement of green growth (green growth indicators; OECD, 2011). This approach has been explored and adapted by countries to track their own progress, as well as updated by the OECD for cross-country monitoring (OECD, 2017b). It has also served as a reference point in joint work of four leading international organisations in the area of green growth (GGKP, 2014; Narloch et al. 2016).

The OECD's green growth indicators are conceived around a production function concept. They focus on the sustainability of "inputs" – such as the natural asset base and sink functions of the environment - and the delivery of "outputs" - the socio-economic conditions and the so-called environmental quality of life: environmental services and amenities related to health and well-being. The ability to turn "inputs" into "outputs" is covered by indicators of productivity and efficiency. Finally, these are supplemented by indicators of policies, efforts and opportunities. In each category, work is ongoing to improve or develop actual indicators and their coverage to allow cross-country comparisons. Importantly, the indicator sets are focussed on a country-level, aiming at national policy makers and the policy tools they have at hand.[5]

Box 2.1. Aggregate green growth metrics

There exists no single broadly accepted measure of environmental performance that could be used for the *Going for Growth* exercise. Attempts to measure environmental performance and sustainability have taken various forms, most commonly variations of "green" GDP (GDP adjusted for environmental degradation) and composite aggregates of diverse indicators of sustainability. Examples include the Yale Environmental Performance Index, UNEPs Green Economy Progress Index, FEEM's Sustainability Index, World Bank's Adjusted Net Savings and Total wealth including produced and natural capital, etc. (for a review see Narloch et al. 2016). All these indicators stumble over the fact of aggregating indicators on diverse phenomena and effects which are not very well measured for a start and on which no straightforward aggregation exists, as for most of them, no market prices can be observed. The weights are based either on arbitrary judgements or on various valuation attempts, but generally are rather controversial. Other important weaknesses include the selection of criteria to be (or not to be) included, inadequate dealing with intertemporal (and distributional) effects and trade-offs, and the pure challenge of measurement of many of the issues.

2.2.1. Environmental performance – assets and productivity

In the absence of a straightforward metric to compare the differing aspects of green growth performance can be assessed on individual dimensions. Cross-country indicators seem most developed for measuring progress on reducing greenhouse gas emissions related to combatting climate change and the global future costs and risks associated with it, and on air pollution. The coverage and usefulness is best for OECD and major emerging market economies (EMEs) covered in *Going for Growth.* In other areas, such as waste, water abstraction and pollution, and biodiversity, indicators are less well developed, though notable progress has recently been made on land cover. In general, across many environmental domains the measurement of flows tends to be better developed than the measurement of quantity and quality of stocks.

Climate change: greenhouse gas emissions

Globally, greenhouse gas (GHG) emissions[6] have continued on an upward trend throughout the 2000s, increasing by around 40% since 1990.[7] They grew less rapidly than world GDP, which roughly doubled in the same time period. In the OECD, absolute emissions peaked around 2005, and are now back to the level of the mid-1990s. Only a handful of countries did not observe falls by 2014.

More recent estimates are available for CO_2 emissions from fuel combustion, with indications that they have remained flat over 2014-16 and possibly even peaked globally (IEA, 2017). Most OECD countries and large emerging market economies have seen their GDP growth exceed emissions growth since the mid-1990s (Figure 2.2, relative decoupling). Moreover, in half of OECD countries, Russia and Lithuania, emissions have shrunk over this period, despite economic growth (Figure 2.2, absolute decoupling).

At the same time, only 12 OECD countries actually decreased the carbon emissions of their consumption basket, indicating that in other countries the fall in domestic emissions was offset by an increase in emissions embodied in imports consumed. In a few cases, such consumption-related emissions showed no decoupling at all: Norway, Indonesia, Turkey, Chile, Saudi Arabia, Brazil and Mexico.

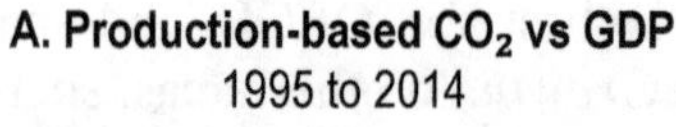

Figure 2.2. Most countries have increased GDP faster than CO_2 emissions[1]

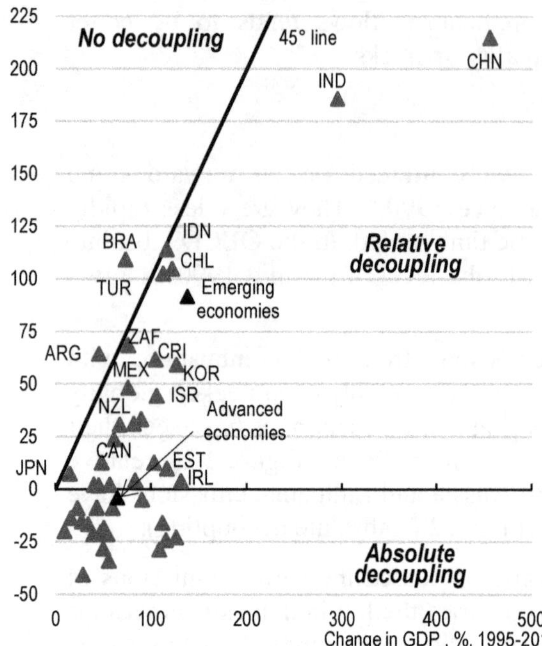

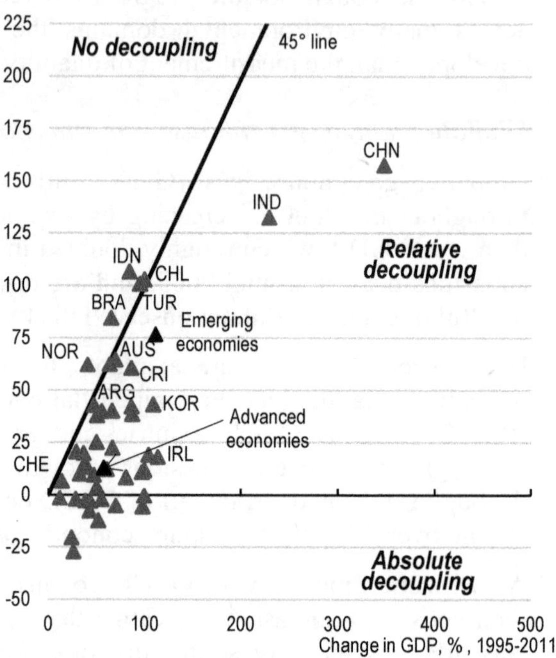

1. Production-based emissions account for the emissions directly "generated" by domestic production. Demand-based indicators account for emissions "used" or "generated" by domestic final demand (the "footprint" approach). They include environmental flows that are embodied in imports, and deduct the environmental flows embodied in exports. The resulting indicators provide insights into the net (direct and indirect) environmental flows resulting from household and government consumption and investment (final domestic demand). Advanced economies refer to OECD countries plus Lithuania and excluding Chile, Mexico and Turkey. Emerging economies refer to Argentina, Brazil, Chile, China, Colombia, Costa Rica, India, Indonesia, Mexico, the Russian Federation, South Africa and Turkey.
Source: OECD (2017), Green Growth Indicators 2017.

StatLink http://dx.doi.org/10.1787/888933680229

Trends in so-called carbon productivity (or the inverse, carbon intensity) reflect jointly: shifts in the industrial structure (e.g. to less energy intensive services), in energy efficiency and in the energy supply mix. Total energy consumption continued to increase in most countries, though more slowly than GDP. While the energy supply mix has been undergoing some changes in the recent years, the share of renewables somewhat increased in the advanced economies, while it fell in most emerging market economies where the supply of coal held up strongly (Figure 2.3).

Figure 2.3. Energy supply remains dominated by fossil fuels

Contributions to total primary energy supply (TPES),[1] 1990-2015

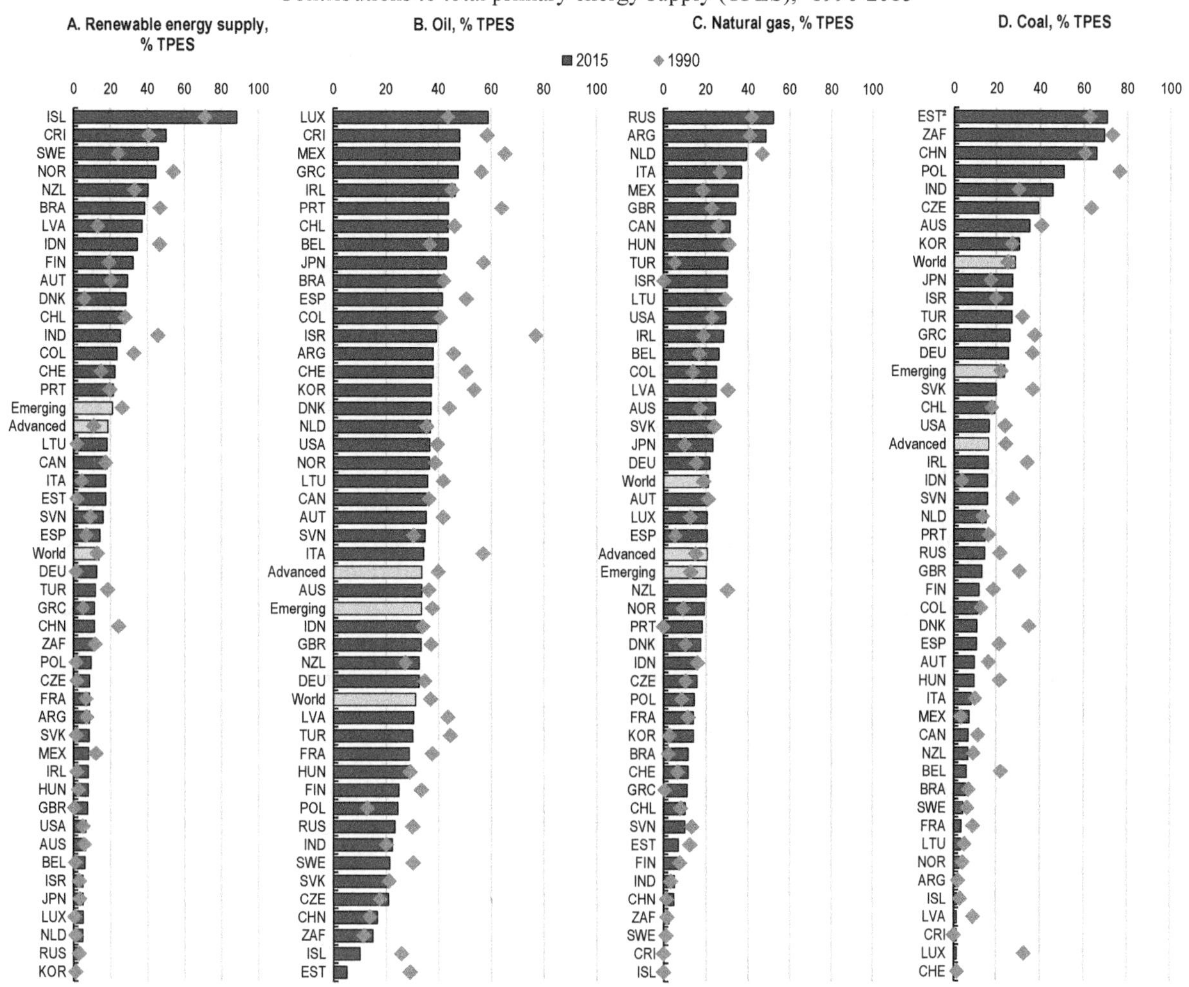

1. Total primary energy supply (TPES) is defined as energy production plus energy imports, minus energy exports, minus international bunkers, then plus or minus stock changes. Advanced economies refer to OECD countries plus Lithuania and excluding Chile, Mexico and Turkey. Emerging economies refer to Argentina, Brazil, Chile, China, Colombia, Costa Rica, India, Indonesia, Mexico, the Russian Federation, South Africa and Turkey.
2. Coal includes oil shale for Estonia

Source: OECD (2017), Green Growth Indicators 2017.

StatLink http://dx.doi.org/10.1787/888933680248

Performance on GHG emissions, their structure and sources can guide abatement policy priorities in reform areas such as taxes, infrastructure investment or innovation. Since effects of climate change bear no direct relation to domestic emissions, the link to domestic economic growth can be made via performance with respect to potential targets – carbon budgets established domestically or committed to in international accords (such as the Paris Agreement of 2015). While in practice national commitments may be vague and difficult to compare, the idea would generally be that the further a country is from a target (such as, zero emissions by a given year), the higher the need for mitigation policy action. At the same time, an adaptation dimension can be taken into consideration, even if climate risk indicators seem somewhat less well developed.[8] Ideally such indicators would address the importance of adaptation policy action, for instance in infrastructure investment or land use planning. At the moment, examples of risks indicators include the share of population living in areas prone to flooding (e.g. for example measured as below 5 meters of elevation; CIESIN, 2013) and the costs and occurrences of extreme weather events, etc.

Air pollution

Air pollution is often labelled as the single biggest environment-related health risk across the globe (WHO, 2014). According to estimates, each year roughly 4 million people die prematurely due to air pollution, the leading environmentally related cause of death (OECD, 2016a). Fine particulate matter ($PM_{2.5}$) undermines populations' well-being through exposure-related increases of risks of heart disease, stroke and respiratory diseases and infections (WHO, 2016; Burnett et al. 2015). Adverse health impacts imply lower productivity, absenteeism and higher medical bills. With no additional policy reaction, by 2060 the impacts of outdoor air pollution are projected to reach 1.5 % of GDP in market impacts, lowering GDP by the equivalent amount. However, air pollution has much higher costs than pure GDP as the overall welfare costs are expected to be much higher. Pollution-related premature deaths are expected to continue increasing to 6-9 million people annually by 2060 (simulated premature deaths attributed to particulate matter and ozone; OECD, 2016a). The effects are estimated to total an equivalent of 9-12 % of GDP when considering non-market effects such as premature deaths, pain and suffering.[9]

A price tag for air pollution may be telling to a broader audience but the cost estimates are typically based on strong assumptions about underlying elements such as how one values an extra year of life. Hence to facilitate monitoring progress, two more direct sets of indicators of air pollution – concentrations and emissions - can be identified and used in combination.

Indicators focusing on concentrations and population exposure can show the gravity of the problem more directly. Different types of pollutants will have different effects, and effects are likely to be non-linear. Green growth indicators include population exposure to fine particles ($PM_{2.5}$) with broad country and time coverage (Figure 2.4). The situation seems worst in the most heavily populated large emerging market economies, but a number of OECD countries are also performing poorly. At the same time, the largest improvements since 1998 were observed in Indonesia, Mexico, Brazil, the United States and Denmark. The exposure to air pollution by ozone measured in EU countries has shown little improvement and NO_2 concentrations in many European cities exceed established limits (OECD, 2016a).

Figure 2.4. Population exposure to air pollution[1]

Average population exposure and share of population exposed by WHO thresholds, PM 2.5

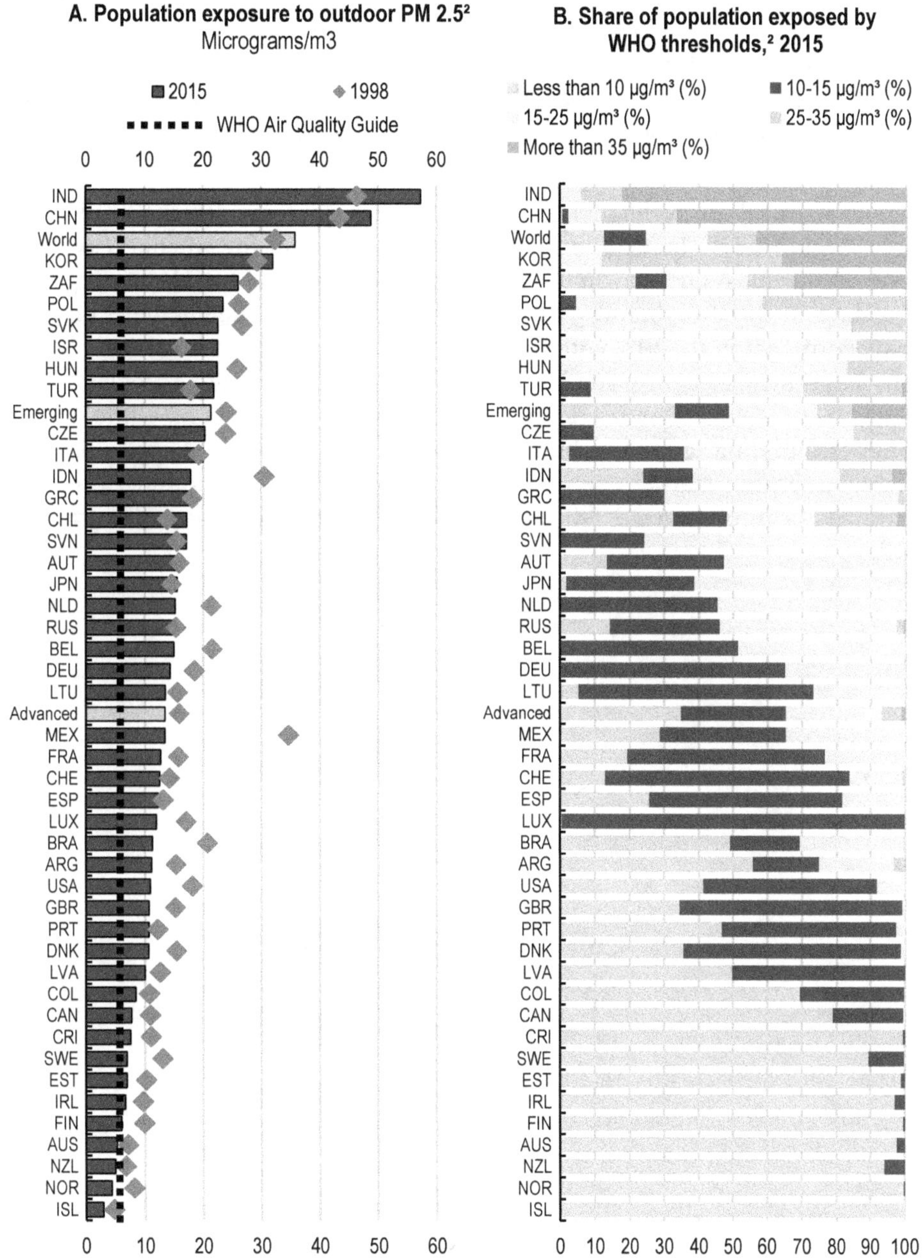

1. The estimates of chronic outdoor exposure to PM2.5 (from both anthropogenic and natural sources) are derived from satellite observations, chemical transport models and ground monitoring stations. They are measured in micrograms per cubic metre. Population exposure to air pollution is calculated by weighting concentrations with populations in each cell of the underlying gridded data.

2. Advanced economies refer to OECD countries plus Lithuania and excluding Chile, Mexico and Turkey. Emerging economies refer to Argentina, Brazil, Chile, China, Colombia, Costa Rica, India, Indonesia, Mexico, the Russian Federation, South Africa and Turkey.

Source: OECD (2017), Green Growth Indicators 2017.

StatLink http://dx.doi.org/10.1787/888933680267

Concentrations are a result of both man-made and natural sources (e.g. due to mineral dust or salt spray), both domestic and possibly foreign (cross-border), as well as the geophysical characteristics of the location (e.g. weather, urban structure). The impacts on health will further depend on the physical distribution of populations as well as the over-time nature of pollution (e.g. long-term vs. peak exposure). Hence, from the policy makers' point of view it is useful to also look at domestic (local) emissions, which can be more directly targeted with mitigation policies than concentrations.

Emissions of harmful air pollutants have seen a sharp decrease since 1990 in the OECD as a whole (Figure 2.5). The data is less well developed than for greenhouse gasses, with good coverage for most OECD (up to 2014) and EU countries, and shorter series for non-OECD, ending in 2010 or before (EDGAR). Progress in reducing these emissions has been most significant in the EU, with emissions well below 1990s levels on all pollutants. Emissions have increased in Canada (PM_{10}), Australia (NO_x, SO_x), Iceland (SO_x, CO, NMVOCs), New Zealand and Turkey (practically all pollutants), Chile and Mexico (NO_x). Interestingly, these tend to be the countries with the highest emission intensities. As for large emerging market economies and other non-OECD countries, only relative decoupling has been observed 1990-2010, with emissions increasing albeit more slowly than GDP.

Figure 2.5. Evolution of emissions of selected air pollutants

Selected countries, relative to 1990

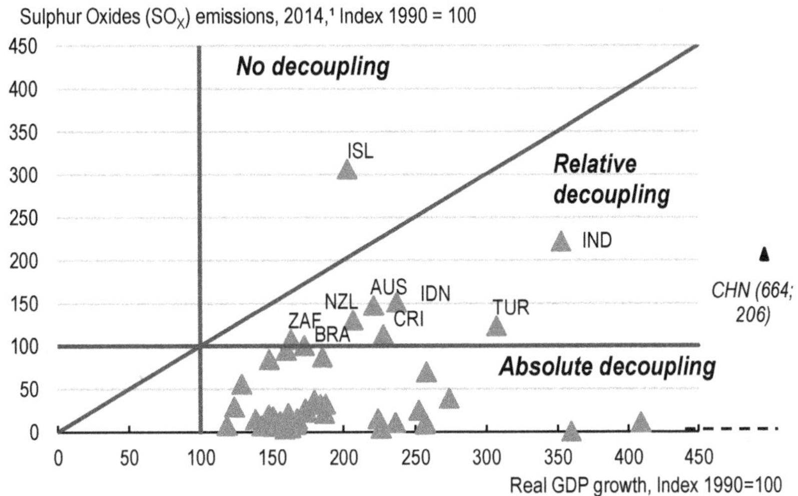

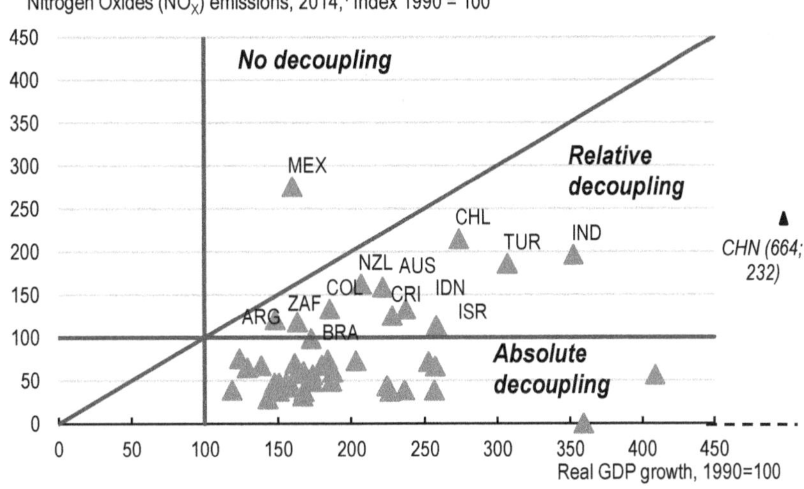

1. Data refer to 2009 for Argentina, Brazil, Chile, China, Colombia, Costa Rica, India, Indonesia, Mexico, South Africa; 2011 for Israel; 2012 for the Russian Federation.

Source: OECD, Air and Climate and Economic Outlook Databases.

StatLink http://dx.doi.org/10.1787/888933680286

Land cover, land use and biodiversity

In the case of land cover, forest resources or biodiversity, the relationship with growth and well-being is particularly complex and often not very well established. Valuation methods used to attribute economic value to such resources are highly imperfect and trade-offs may be inevitable, in particular in the short term. For example, forest resources may be assessed by the value of timber – a very narrow approach, which does not take into account their role for biodiversity, air quality or erosion. The measured direct contribution of forestry and logging to GDP is hence modest in advanced economies – typically below 0.5% of GDP - with the exception of some countries with large forest endowments (and low population density) such as Finland, Latvia, New Zealand,

Sweden, Estonia, Chile and Canada – but even there forestry contributes well below 2% of GDP. At the same time, the GDP contribution of down-stream industries involved wood-based manufacturing is several times higher. Data for emerging economies is of poorer coverage, but in the large emerging market economies the export contribution of forest products is also small.

Land cover changes are used as an indication of pressures on the natural environment, among them, on biodiversity. In fact, land cover change is the leading contributor to (non-marine) biodiversity loss (CBD, 2010). In light of this, the OECD has recently moved the frontier on indicators of land cover changes and conversions (OECD, 2017d). The new set is based on satellite images and has broad coverage – OECD and G20 countries (as well as regions) – and is designed for tracking land cover changes and conversions over a longer time horizon, starting in the 1990s.

Globally, some 2.7% of natural and semi-natural land has been lost since 1992,[10] with the largest losses in Brazil, China, Russia, the United States and Indonesia – i.e. among the largest and most populated, but also most biodiverse countries (OECD, 2017d). OECD countries have lost on average 1.4% of natural land, with a wide dispersion ranging from 0% to 16% (Figure 2.6). Land use cover changes generally follow a standard path related to development - the conversion of natural land to cropland, and some of it eventually to urban (or built-up) land. Among advanced economies three quarters of natural land lost was lost to cropland. In emerging market economies, the figure was significantly higher. About 2% of total cropland was converted to urban land globally, though the individual country figures did not seem closely related to demographic pressures.

Figure 2.6. Losses in natural and semi-natural land[1]

Selected countries, relative to 1992

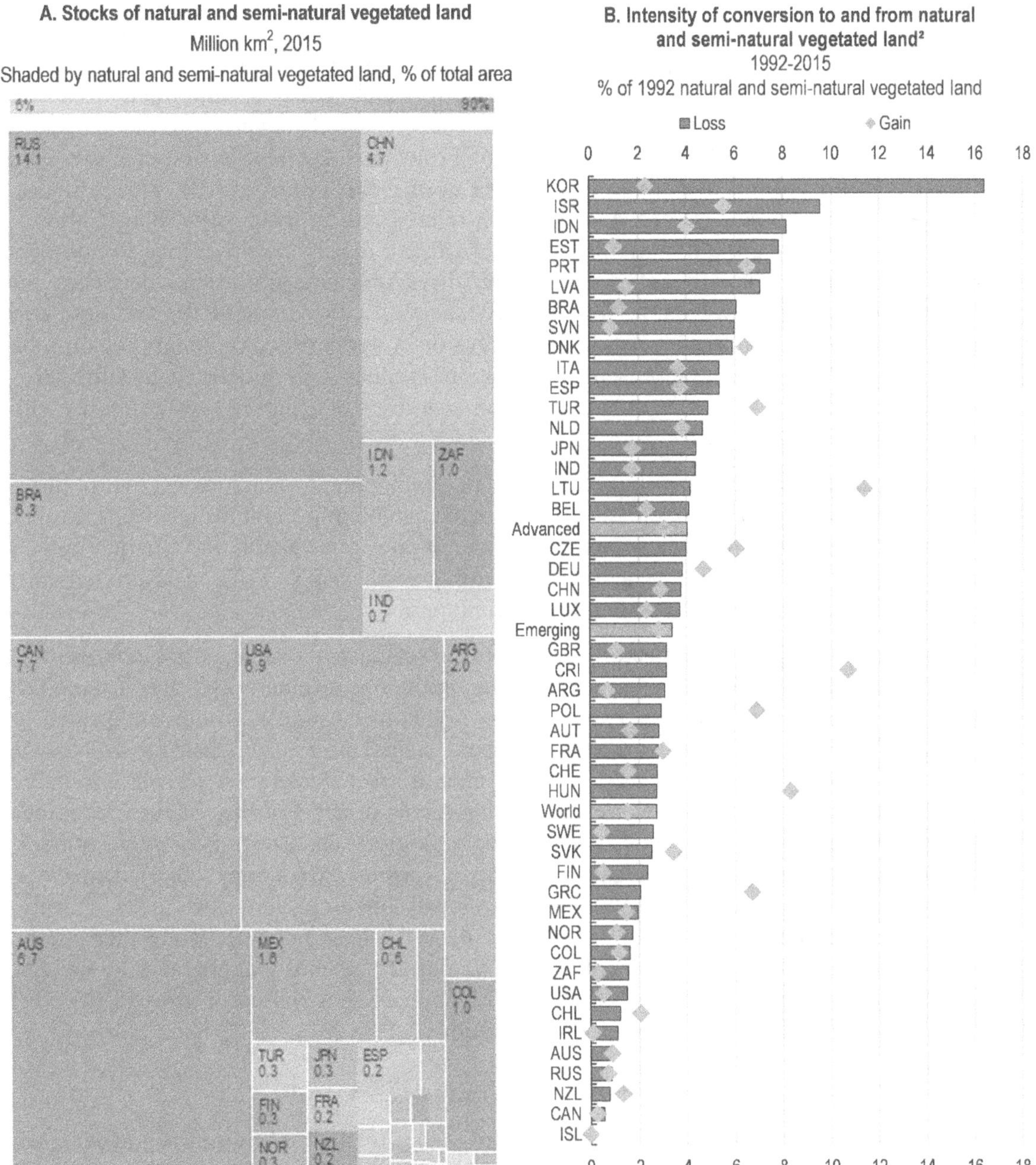

1. World figures refer to the area within political boundaries (excluding seas, oceans and Antarctica).
2. Advanced economies refer to OECD countries plus Lithuania and excluding Chile, Mexico and Turkey. Emerging economies refer to Argentina, Brazil, Chile, China, Colombia, Costa Rica, India, Indonesia, Mexico, the Russian Federation, South Africa and Turkey.

Source: *Land cover change and conversions: Methodology and results for OECD and G20 countries*, forthcoming.

StatLink http://dx.doi.org/10.1787/888933680305

Other indicators of environmental performance

Indicators on waste, waste water treatment and water efficiency, as well as on water pollution and scarcity are less well developed, and unlikely to be suitable for systematic use in *Going for Growth* at this point. Waste data suffer from comparability problems, and good available data tends to focus on municipal waste only. Water abstraction is partly determined by geographical and metrological conditions and is rarely available with information on the post-abstraction use – which can be important from the environmental point of view. Water quality is relatively well covered by the European Environmental Agency, the US Environmental Protection Agency, but comparable data across countries are not available. The case is even weaker for discharges of pollution into water. The specific case of water pollution-related indicators specific to agriculture - nutrient balances (relative to agricultural land surface), that is the difference in nutrients inputs leaving farms (mainly as manure and fertilisers) relative to nutrients necessary for crop and forage – are available for most EU and OECD countries for the past two decades. In general, while pure national averages on water scarcity or quality may not be very telling, such data can be presented with more emphasis on outliers, e.g. with shares of agricultural activities in area subject to water scarcity risks, share of water bodies with substandard pollution levels, etc.

Environment-related indicators linked closely to development – such as access to clean, safe water, sanitation or a reliable electricity source can be important for emerging market economies. Poor performance on such categories implies poor health and life quality and exclusion for many and can be a bottleneck for growth and well-being improvements. Such data is available annually over a longer time period.

Finally, sets of aggregate indicators on natural asset bases – such as natural resource indexes and related non-energy material consumption and productivity - are designed to show the reliance on and the exhaustibility of non-renewable resources (primarily underground minerals). However, at the current stage, their usefulness for *Going for Growth* is disputable. Firstly, the estimates of natural asset stocks have proven unreliable – for example due to new discoveries or varying levels of accessibility of such resources (both across countries and time, due to technological changes). Secondly, mineral resources are internationally tradeable (and to a various extent recyclable); hence the reliance on them as inputs for growth is not obviously linked to domestic stocks. Thirdly, the aggregation methods are often problematic or at the least not well established – e.g., for material productivity, materials of various values are generally aggregated by weight. As for reliance on mining and exporting such resources as a source of growth, EAMFP growth provides a general, even if crude, indication.

2.2.2. Indicators of efforts, opportunities and policies

Green growth indicators also cover a set of indicators related to environmental policies, efforts and opportunities. The overall idea is to compare country policy stances (and intermediate outcomes, such as innovation) – in order to assess efforts in preserving a clean environment. However, the challenge of measuring and comparing environmental policies comes in as a key factor limiting the development of such indicators.

Indicators most closely related to policy focus on the stringency of the environmental policy signal. The indicators available include direct measures – OECD's Environmental Policy Stringency (EPS; Botta and Kozluk, 2014) and the perceived stringency of policies, based on responses to the World Economic Forum's (WEF) Executive Opinion Survey. The former focuses on the policy imposed "costs" of polluting – for example a more stringent policy is associated with a higher tax on emissions or tighter pollution standards. The EPS is a *de jure* measure, available for most OECD countries and large emerging market economies since the 1990s till 2015. It is a broad proxy, but currently limited largely to a selection of climate and air pollution policies.[11] The WEF's survey-based measure attempts at overall de facto stringency evaluation (as well as the evaluation of actual enforcement) by asking company managers. It covers practically all countries (Figure 2.7). Both approaches have significant limitations, but can give an indication of the overall stringency of environmental policies in countries.

Figure 2.7. Different proxies of environmental policy stringency

A. Different measures of stringency of environmental policies show a similar picture

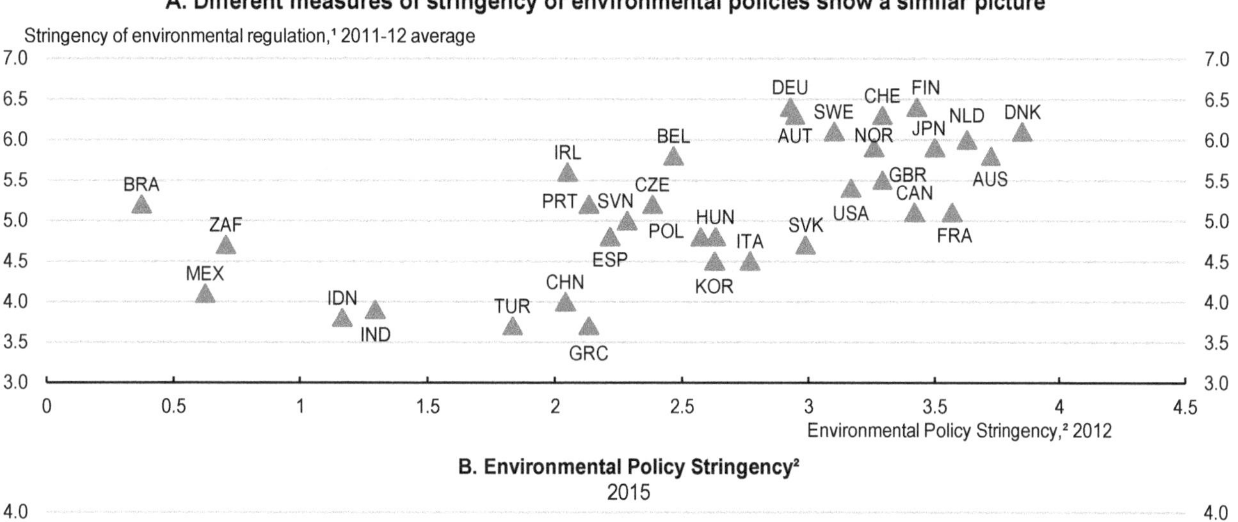

B. Environmental Policy Stringency²
2015

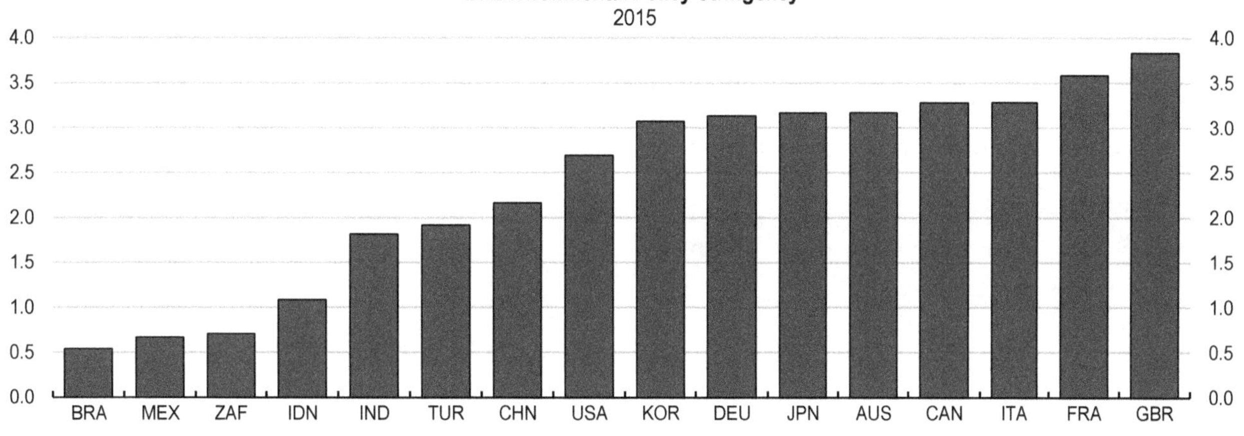

1. Index of 1-7 from least to most restrictive environmental regulations.
2. The OECD Environmental Policy Stringency Index (EPS) is a country-specific and internationally-comparable measure of the stringency of environmental policy. Stringency is defined as the degree to which environmental policies put an explicit or implicit price on polluting or environmentally harmful behaviour. The index ranges from 0 (not stringent) to 6 (highest degree of stringency).

Source: World Economic Forum and OECD, Environmental Policy Database.

StatLink http://dx.doi.org/10.1787/888933680324

On top of this, the OECD also collects data on environmentally-related tax revenues – often used to indicate the potential for generating revenues, though this needs to be treated cautiously, as in principle high environmental tax revenues could not only indicate stringent environmental (pricing) policies, but equally well, large environmental issues.[12] In practice, the majority of revenues come from energy taxation, with motor-vehicle taxation as the second item. Notably, many of these taxes are levied primarily for revenue, rather than environmental purposes. The country coverage of the indicators is gradually increasing beyond the OECD and large emerging market economies (Figure 2.8). More generally, environmentally related tax revenues tend to be below 4 per cent of GDP. They are often argued to have potential to substitute revenues from direct taxes, if the environmental damage associated with the production and consumption of goods and services is more systematically priced. Importantly, if as environmental taxes are increased they also serve their function – i.e. incentivise firms and households to decouple activity from the environment – the tax base should be shrinking over time.

Indicators and proxies more specific to climate policies include OECD's effective carbon prices (OECD, 2016b) – which attempt to show the effective pricing of carbon contents of different fuels (and uses) attributable to taxes and trading schemes in each country. The country coverage is similar as with tax revenues, but time series are not yet available. Final user energy prices are also sometimes used as a proxy for the stringency of climate policies (Sato et al. 2015). Important policy related datasets concern fossil fuel subsidies (OECD Inventory of Support Measures for Fossil Fuels) and producer subsidies to agriculture (OECD, 2017c) - as both fossil fuel combustion and intensive agriculture have direct links to environmental challenges.

Notably, some of the tax-related policy indicators already serve for identification for pro-growth priorities in *Going for Growth.* Many countries with a priority to shift the tax structure to consumption (or specifically environmental) taxes raise a rather low share of revenues from environmental taxation (Figure 2.8). At the same time, countries with a priority to reduce tax expenditures or broaden the tax base tend to have intermediate levels of such exemptions supporting fossil fuels (Figure 2.9).

Figure 2.8. Large variations in share of revenues from environmentally-related taxation among countries with a *Going for Growth* priority to shift the tax structure[1]

Percentage of total tax revenue, 2014

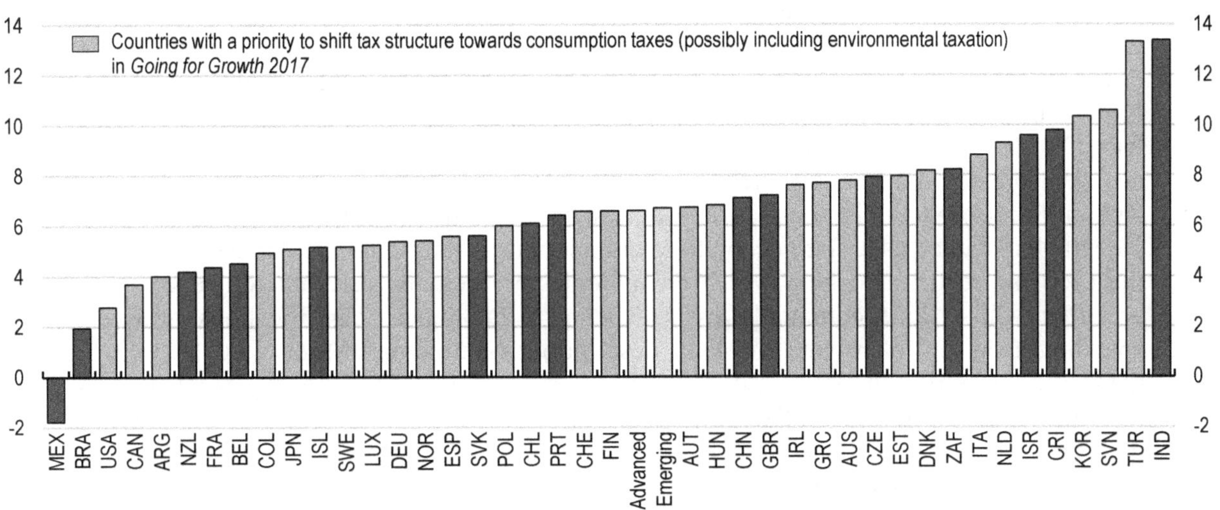

1. Advanced economies refer to OECD countries plus Lithuania and excluding Chile, Mexico and Turkey. Emerging economies refer to Argentina, Brazil, Chile, China, Colombia, Costa Rica, India, Indonesia, Mexico, the Russian Federation, South Africa and Turkey. Data refer to 2013 for Australia, Brazil, Colombia, Japan, Mexico, the Netherlands, Poland; 2000 for Greece.
Source: OECD, Environmental Policy Database.

StatLink http://dx.doi.org/10.1787/888933680343

Figure 2.9. Fossil fuel subsidies versus recommendations to reduce tax expenditures

Percentage of total tax revenue, 2014

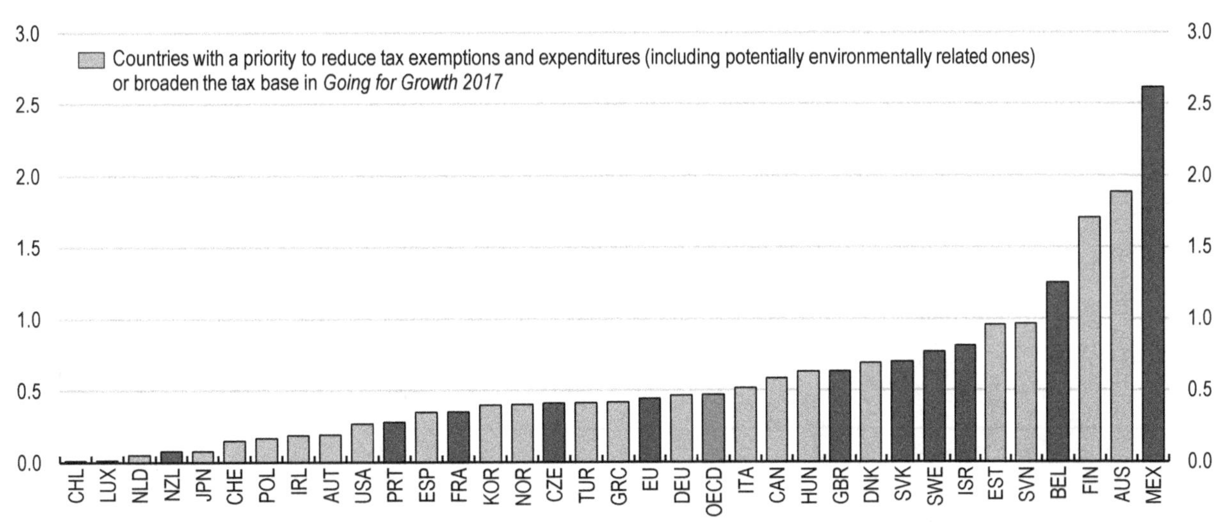

Source: OECD, Green Growth Database.

StatLink http://dx.doi.org/10.1787/888933680362

"Green" innovation

Indicators of "green" innovation constitute an attempt to capture the "intermediate" step of the green growth transformation – the development of new, more environmentally friendly ways of producing and consuming. Innovation is a necessary condition for green growth – it is the means of reducing the negative effects of growth and well-being on the environment and hence increasing their long-term sustainability and resilience. Innovation-related indicators are either input-based such as R&D spending or output-based, such as data derived from patent counts (Figure 2.10 and Figure 2.11). While well accepted proxies, neither is perfect – the link between innovation spending and actual technological progress is complex and only a fraction of innovations are patented and patentable. Neither takes into account actual adoption. Additional challenges arise from the problem of distinguishing which technologies are actually relevant for progress on green growth – done commonly by reviewing technological classifications of R&D spending areas and of patents and their descriptions (Hascic and Migoto, 2015). OECD data relies primarily on technology classifications, with specific technologies labelled as relevant for the environment. Patent data cannot directly answer the question of which of the innovations or inventions are actually important, but they have key advantages: wide availability (across time and countries) and their quantitative nature.

Overall, while government support to R&D labelled as energy- and environment-related has generally kept up or increased in most OECD countries throughout 2000s, patenting in so-called green technologies seems to have slowed globally relative to a surge in the earlier 2000s. The vast majority of green inventions originate in the advanced economies, particularly in large economies with high overall R&D spending and often stringent environmental policy signals - such as the United States, Japan, Germany, Korea and France. Denmark, while a smaller contributor in absolute terms, leads in terms of share of green patents. The large emerging market economies, in particular China and India, have noted rapid increase though still contribute less in absolute value relative to their size.

Figure 2.10. Government R&D expenditure relevant for green growth

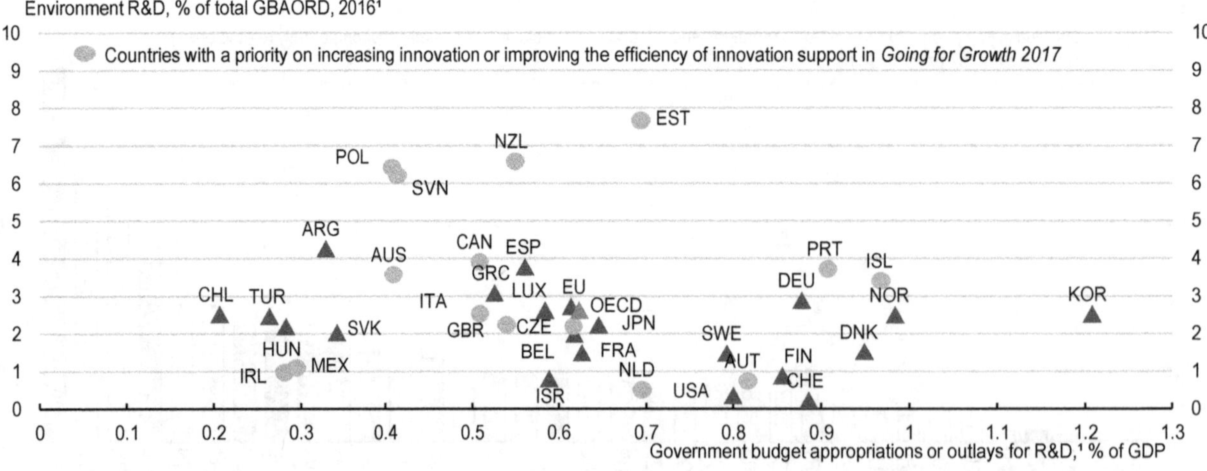

1. GBAORD refers to Government budget appropriations or outlays for R&D. The last available year is 2017 for Austria and the Netherlands; 2015 for Belgium, Chile, Spain, Estonia, the United Kingdom, Greece, Hungary, Ireland, Israel, Italy, Korea, Poland, Slovenia, Sweden, Turkey and the Russian Federation; 2014 for Switzerland and Iceland; 2013 for Canada; 2012 for Argentina.

Source: OECD, Innovation in Environment-related technologies Database; OECD, Science, Technology and Patents Database and OECD, Economic Outlook Database.

StatLink http://dx.doi.org/10.1787/888933680381

Figure 2.11. Share of patenting in so-called environmental technologies[1]

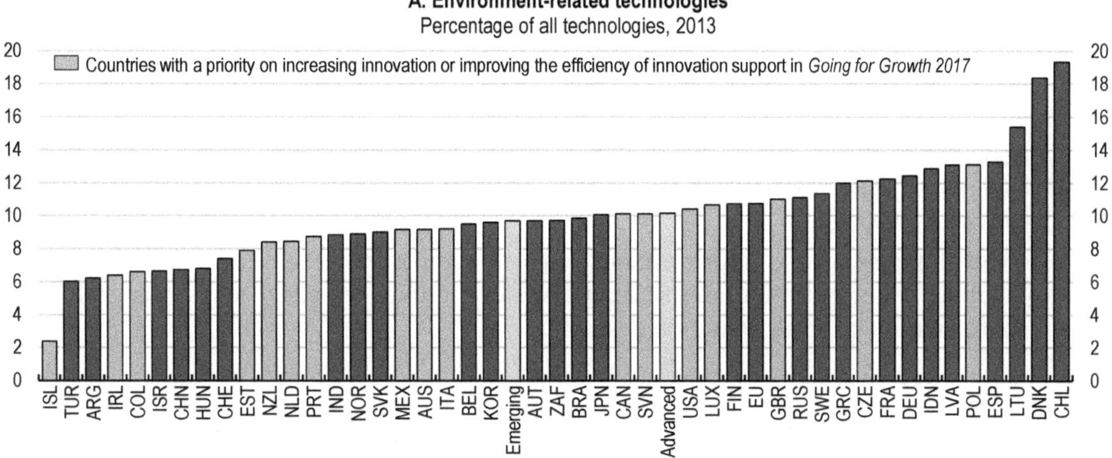

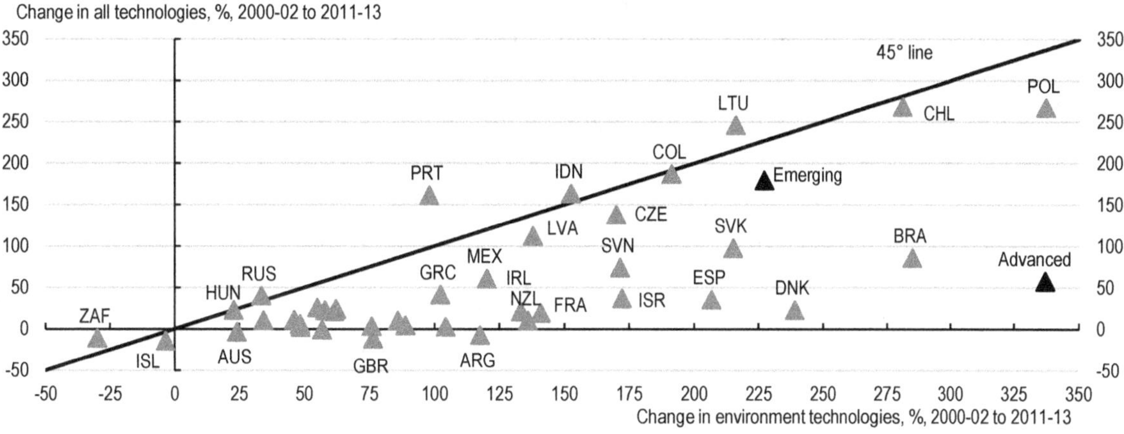

1. Advanced economies refer to OECD countries plus Lithuania and excluding Chile, Mexico and Turkey. Emerging economies refer to Argentina, Brazil, Chile, China, Colombia, Costa Rica, India, Indonesia, Mexico, the Russian Federation, South Africa and Turkey.

Source: OECD, Innovation in Environment-related technologies Database and OECD (2017), Green Growth Indicators 2017.

StatLink http://dx.doi.org/10.1787/888933680400

2.3. Gaps in green growth measurement - what would we like to measure (better)?

The recent progress on green growth indicators allows a first step in the direction of integrating green growth into *Going for Growth.* A detailed proposal for such an integration is underway, but the process will inevitably be gradual and cautious – proceeding as work on green growth indicators progresses. Information on some of the key indicators is summarised in Annex Table 2.A.1. Several milestones would improve the potential for such integration:

Indicators:

- The coverage and timeliness of many green growth indicators needs to be improved. The fact that in key environmental areas long-term trend developments are more important than short term fluctuations is not per se problematic for *Going for Growth* which also focuses on the medium to longer run. However, to better detect progress or turning points, more up-to-date information may be desirable, e.g. for exposures and risks, GHGs or some of the policy variables. More generally coverage of a broader set of countries and intermediate years will always be welcome.
- New dimensions and improvements (e.g. on comparability) of existing indicators such as water pollution and scarcity, waste, biodiversity and ecosystems and in particular on policies would be desirable.

Concepts:

- Improved treatment of global goods (climate, oceans, biodiversity) and their incorporation in national objectives. As such targets are often outside of the direct responsibility of domestic policy makers, incorporation into *Going for Growth* could benefit from developing indicators such as the distance from a countries ambition, e.g. measured by long-term international commitments (e.g. carbon budgets that could be based on COP 21).
- Improved coverage of local or regional environmental issues and of risks that are not a central scenario. As such, these may be less evidently linked to overall growth and well-being, especially in large countries, but their importance may be better covered in moving towards indicators of population (or economy) exposures to risks (GDP at risk, population living in areas with higher health risks, agricultural production in areas at risk of flooding or water scarcity, etc.)
- Better measurement of how country environmental policies compare – in terms of stringency and other aspects of design (flexibility, stability, growth-friendliness).

Empirical evidence:

- Stronger empirical evidence linking: (i) environmental damage to economic growth and well-being (both direct and via increased risks); (ii) environmental policies to economic, well-being and environmental outcomes; (iii) economic policies and outcomes to pressures on the environment; over various time horizons would allow more directly targeting the *Going for Growth* objective of strong, sustainable growth and more concrete formulation of policy recommendations.
- Translating this evidence into better indicators of risks, costs of environmental damage and using it e.g. to inform weighting in the construction of aggregate indicators.

Endnotes

3. A key input into this chapter is the OECD work on Green Growth Indicators, led by the Environment Directorate in co-operation with the Statistics Directorate (OECD, 2017b; http://oe.cd/ggi).

4. Detailed information on the OECD's Environmentally Adjusted Multi-factor Productivity (EAMFP) measure can be found in Cardenas Rodriguez et al. (2016) and Brandt et al. (2014).

5. In some cases, more disaggregated data, e.g. at regional or city level are available.

6. Excluding land use, land use change and forestry (LULUCF).

7. The latest world observation is 2012. For OECD and large EMEs, the latest data is 2014.

8. There is work planned in 2018-19 at the OECD on developing indicators in this area.

9. The OECD (2016a) work provides a global outlook to 2060 for the major impacts of increased air pollution on human health and agriculture: numbers of premature deaths, cases of illness and loss of agricultural yields. It uses a detailed general equilibrium modelling framework, the OECD's ENV-Linkages model, to calculate regional and global economic costs related to those impacts that can be linked to markets, such as changes in health care expenditures, labour productivity, and agricultural production. Non-market impacts, such as the premature deaths and the costs of pain and suffering from illness, are derived using estimates of willingness-to-pay (WTP) based on direct valuation studies. The welfare costs of the premature deaths caused by air pollution are calculated using the value of a statistical life (VSL).

10. Natural and semi-natural land is used to define land covered by natural or semi-natural vegetation with limited anthropogenic footprint.

11. The OECD collects a large number of details on existing policies in the Database on Policy Instruments for Environment (PINE) http://www2.oecd.org/ecoinst/queries/. In particular, the EPS makes use of this data.

12. OECD defines environmentally related taxes as any taxes (or other pricing instruments, such as tradeable permits) levied on environmentally relevant tax-bases, such as emissions to air or water, energy sources and energy sources, motor vehicles, waste, etc.

References

Acemoglu D. et al. (2012), The Environment and Directed Technical Change, American Economic Review 2012, 102(1): 131–166. http://dx.doi=10.1257/aer.102.1.131

Albrizio S. et al. (2014), Do environmental policies matter for productivity growth? Insights from new cross-country measures of environmental policies, OECD Economics Department Working Paper No. 1176. OECD Publishing, Paris. http://dx.doi.org/10.1787/18151973

Botta, E. and T. Koźluk (2014), "Measuring Environmental Policy Stringency in OECD Countries: A Composite Index Approach", OECD Economics Department Working Papers, No. 1177, OECD Publishing, Paris. http://dx.doi.org/10.1787/5jxrjnc45gvg-en

Brandt N., P. Schreyer and V. Zipperer (2014), "Productivity Measurement with Natural Capital and Bad Outputs", http://doi.org/bb5z

Burnett, R.T. et al. (2014), "An integrated risk function for estimating the global burden of disease attributable to ambient fine particulate matter exposure", Environmental Health Perspectives, 122: 397-403.

Cárdenas Rodríguez M., Haščič I. and Souchier M. (2016), "Environmentally adjusted multifactor productivity: methodology and empirical results for OECD and G20 countries", http://doi.org/bqw9

CBD (2010), Global Biodiversity Outlook 3, Convention on Biological Diversity, www.cbd.int/gbo3.

CIESIN (2016), Gridded Population of the World, version 4 (GPWv4), Center for International Earth Science Information Network, http://dx.doi.org/10.7927/H4X63JVC. http://sedac.ciesin.columbia.edu/data/set/lecz-urban-rural-population-land-area-estimates-v2

Haščič, I. and M. Migotto (2015), "Measuring environmental innovation using patent data", OECD Environment Working Papers, No. 89, OECD Publishing, Paris. http://dx.doi.org/10.1787/5js009kf48xw-en

IEA (2017), "IEA finds CO_2 emissions flat for thirds straight year even as global economy grew in 2016", https://www.iea.org/newsroom/news/2017/march/iea-finds-co2-emissions-flat-for-third-straight-year-even-as-global-economy-grew.html

Koźluk, T. (2014), "The Indicators of the Economic Burdens of Environmental Policy Design: Results from the OECD Questionnaire", OECD Economics Department Working Papers, No. 1178, OECD Publishing, Paris. http://dx.doi.org/10.1787/5jxrjnbnbm8v-en

Narloch, U, Kozluk, T, Lloyd, A .(2016), "Measuring Inclusive Green Growth at the Country Level, Taking Stock of Measurement Approaches and Indicators" Green Growth Knowledge Platform Working Paper 02 2016, GGKP Research Committee on Measurement & Indicators. http://www.greengrowthknowledge.org/sites/default/files/downloads/resource/Measuring_Inclusive_Green_Growth_at_the_Country_Level.pdf

OECD (2011), Towards Green Growth, OECD Publishing, Paris. http://dx.doi.org/10.1787/9789264111318-en

OECD (2016a), The Economic Consequences of Outdoor Air Pollution, OECD Publishing, Paris. http://dx.doi.org/10.1787/9789264257474-en

OECD (2016b), Effective Carbon Rates: Pricing CO_2 through Taxes and Emissions Trading Systems, OECD Publishing, Paris. http://dx.doi.org/10.1787/9789264260115-en

OECD (2017a), *Going for Growth* 2017, OECD Publishing, Paris. http://dx/doi.org/10.1787/growth-2017-en

OECD (2017b), Green Growth Indicators 2017, OECD Publishing, Paris. http://dx.doi.org/10.1787/9789264268586-en

OECD (2017c), Agricultural Policy Monitoring and Evaluation 2017, OECD Publishing, Paris. http://dx.doi.org/10.1787/agr_pol-2017-en

OECD (2017d) Land Cover Change and Conversions: Methodology and Results for OECD and G20 Countries, Document prepared for the 23-24 November 2017 Meeting of the Working Party on Environmental Information (ENV/EPOC/WPEI(2017)/3)

Sato, M., Singer, G., Dussaux, D., & Lovo, S. (2015). International and sectoral variation in energy prices 1995-2011: how does it relate to emissions policy stringency? Centre for Climate Change Economics and Policy Working Paper, (212).

WHO (2014), 7 million premature deaths annually linked to air pollution, Media Centre News release, World Health Organization, Geneva, www.who.int/mediacentre/news/releases/2014/airpollution/en/.

Annex 2.A. List of selected available green growth indicators and coverage

Annex Table 2.A.1. Selected green growth indicators with potential for inclusion in *Going for Growth*

Indicator area	Coverage and availability	Relevance for *Going for Growth* pro-growth priority areas and recommendations	Remarks
Performance: Climate change			
GHG emissions (total economy)	GHGs: model based estimates are global. Actual data – primarily for developed countries. Updates frequent, but coverage worse for LULUCF. CO_2 from combustion: global coverage, annual updates, up to date.	Taxation, infrastructure, land use, agriculture and transport (emissions by sector)	CO_2 is available in both emissions linked to "production" and "consumption". Often used in relation to output variables ("carbon productivity"). Performance can be assessed w.r.t. the assumed target of reducing emissions to zero eventually. Various supporting indicators (e.g. on energy mix) are available.
Carbon budgets	At the moment not well developed.	Taxation, infrastructure, land use, agriculture and transport (emissions by sector)	Important but unlikely useful at this stage.
Adaptation and risks	Poor and often out of date, particularly in the case of exposures and risks. Work planned in the OECD Environment Directorate 2018-19.	Taxation, infrastructure, land use, agriculture and transport (emissions by sector)	Important but unlikely useful at this stage.
Performance: Air pollution			
Air pollution concentrations (and exposure)	Global coverage of at least two decades for PM. Coverage much poorer for other pollutants – mainly selected cities in developed countries.	Infrastructure/public transport, road pricing, zoning/land regulations	Includes the contribution of natural factors.
Air pollution emissions	Inventory data available by source for 6 main categories of pollutants for OECD countries (up to date and historical).	Infrastructure/public transport, road pricing, zoning/land regulations, taxation	Not necessarily linked to environmental outcomes.

Indicator area	Coverage and availability	Relevance for *Going for Growth* pro-growth priority areas and recommendations	Remarks
	Model-based estimates for totals (on main categories) available for a longer time period globally (up to 2012). Should improve with forthcoming global emission accounts.		
Performance: Natural assets and land use			
Land cover and land cover changes	Global, since 1990s	Zoning, land regulation, Infrastructure/public transport, road pricing	Focus on quantity (not quality) of land cover types. Also available at regional levels.
Land cover conversions	Global, since 1990s	Zoning, land regulation, Infrastructure/public transport, road pricing	Focus on quantity (not quality) of land cover types. Also available at regional levels.
Nitrogen and Phosphorus balances	Primarily OECD, since the 1980s or 1990s	Agricultural subsidies	Not necessarily straightforward to interpret and link directly with policies.
(Intermediate) Performance: Innovation and infrastructure			
"Green" Patents	Global, annual	Innovation policies, taxation (directed technological change)	General limitations of patent data.
Government support to "green" R&D	Limited to energy categories. OECD countries, history available through lags in updating.	Innovation policies, taxation (directed technological change)	Based on general government expenditures in a limited set of categories.
Access to clean water, sanitation, electricity	Available globally, up to date and with history.	Infrastructure, Inclusiveness	Primarily relevant for EMEs.
Policies			
Environmentally related taxation	OECD + selected large EMEs + selected others. Updated annually since 1994.	Tax structure and tax base (exemptions), transport policies	Allows the identification of the structure of taxes, which can be relevant for the formulation of the recommendation. The motivation for the individual taxes is not necessarily environmental (e.g. excise taxes).
Fossil fuel subsidies	OECD and selected large EMEs (OECD). Key EMEs (IEA). Updated since 2000s.	Fossil fuels subsidies, Taxation (broadening tax base)	OECD methodology is based on actual inventories of measures. IEA methodology is based on the gap between domestic

Indicator area	Coverage and availability	Relevance for *Going for Growth* pro-growth priority areas and recommendations	Remarks
			price and global prices.
Producer support to agriculture	OECD. Updated since 1990s. Forthcoming OECD work on harmful fisheries subsidies.	Agricultural subsidies	Disaggregates between producer and consumer support. Total sums, with EU treated as one entity. Can include subsidies for improving environmental performance.
Environmental policy stringency (OECD)	Since 1990s. Most OECD + selected large EMEs. Last update 2012 or 2015 (G20).	General, rule of law, taxation	Very general composite proxy based primarily on air and climate policies.
WEF stringency of environmental policies	Global, annual, since 2000s.	General, rule of law	Problematic over-time comparison, update availability not always clear. Some potential sampling issues.
Indicators of burdens on entry and competition due to environmental policies (BEEP)	2013 only, update planned in 2018. OECD countries + ZAF, HRV.	Barriers to entry and competition, administrative burdens on firms, product market regulation	Limited amount of issues covered, primarily on the design aspects of environmental policies.
Others			
EAMFP	OECD and G20, annual since 1990s	General	Multi factor productivity growth adjusted for selected air pollutants, CO_2 and key mineral resources.

Chapter 3. Policies for productivity: the design of insolvency regimes across countries

This Chapter presents the new OECD indicators of the design of insolvency regimes in light of their relevance for productivity growth and Going for Growth *more generally. It shows significant cross-country differences in the extent to which insolvency regimes promote orderly exit of non-viable firms, indicating that some countries have scope to improve resource allocation and productivity through reforms of bankruptcy laws and procedures.*

The statistical data for Israel are supplied by and under the responsibility of the relevant Israeli authorities. The use of such data by the OECD is without prejudice to the status of the Golan Heights, East Jerusalem and Israeli settlements in the West Bank under the terms of international law.

Main findings

- Poorly performing insolvency regimes can be linked to three inter-related sources of labour productivity weakness: the survival of so-called "zombie" firms – that should otherwise exit the market, and capital misallocation, i.e. the trapping of resources in low productivity uses and stalling technological diffusion
- A new set of OECD indicators on insolvency regimes gathers information on the design of insolvency regimes that are relevant for ensuring the smooth exit or effective restructuring of failing firms, such as: the availability of a fresh start; mechanisms to prevent and streamline insolvency proceedings; the availability of tools related to restructuring; and additional information on the role of courts, provisions distinguishing between honest and fraudulent bankruptcies and the rights of employees.
- The indicators show significant cross-country differences, with the insolvency regime in the United Kingdom entailing relatively low personal costs to failed entrepreneurs and low barriers to restructuring, while containing a number of provisions to aid prevention and streamlining.
- On the other hand, the insolvency regimes in Estonia and Hungary create the highest impediments to a smooth and timely exit or restructuring. The regimes could benefit from lowering costs to failed entrepreneurs, improving the availability of tools for restructuring and improving prevention and streamlining.
- The OECD indicators of insolvency regimes complement the existing World Bank Doing Business indicators of insolvency, through a more complete coverage of the underlying provisions. Moreover, by linking weaknesses more directly to policies they can serve directly to identify country recommendations within the *Going for Growth* framework.
- In *Going for Growth* 2017, six countries - Australia, Estonia, Italy, Poland, Portugal and South Africa - had a priority recommendation to reform bankruptcy laws. In 2017, reforms were undertaken only in Italy. In the future, such recommendations can be fine-tuned using the new OECD indicators.

3.1. Introduction

Recent OECD research on productivity growth has provided renewed evidence on the importance of open and competitive product markets in fostering efficiency gains, innovation and economic growth. It has underscored the importance of promoting the entry of new firms and the redeployment of resources from poorly performing firms to high-productivity ones. Poorly performing firms that are unable to improve should exit the market or restructure so as to free the resources that can be used more productively in better-managed, more innovative firms. Strong competitive pressures and market selection are key mechanisms to make this happen. However, the effectiveness of these mechanisms can be weakened - or strengthened - by various regulations through their influence on firm entry and exit, as well as on the ease of reallocations of capital and labour resources across firms and business sectors.

For many years, the OECD has developed and up-dated an economy-wide indicator of regulatory barriers to firm entry and competition, measuring the stance of product market regulation in an internationally comparable way (Koske et al., 2015). However, a similar indicator of regulatory barriers to firm exit has been lacking. Filling the gap, this chapter presents the new cross-country policy indicators of insolvency regimes for 36 countries, based on countries' responses to a recent OECD questionnaire (Adalet McGowan and Andrews, 2018).[13]

The new OECD indicators cover policies which – based on international experience and research – may carry adverse consequences for productivity growth by delaying the initiation and increasing the length of insolvency proceedings. They have been constructed on the assumption that the inefficiencies on the exit margin are likely to be more pronounced in economies where insolvency regimes impose a high personal cost to failed entrepreneurs or lack sufficient preventative and streamlining measures and tools to facilitate restructuring. They also cover other features that may delay the timely resolution of financial distress, such as the role of courts, employee rights and the treatment of fraudulent activities.

The next section provides a brief reminder of why insolvency regimes matter for productivity growth. Section 3.3 presents the characteristics of an effective insolvency regime. Section 3.4 discusses the measurement of key design aspects, and the respective country performance based on the information collected through the OECD questionnaire. Section 3.4 summarises the new cross-country evidence on the basis of the composite OECD indicator of insolvency regimes.

3.2. Why do insolvency regimes matter for productivity growth?

Creative destruction is a key feature of well-functioning economies. Over the long-run, productivity growth is sustained by firms' experimentation with new ideas, the broad diffusion of advanced technologies and business practices among firms and the reallocation of scarce resources to their most productive uses. There is growing recognition, however, that the labour productivity slowdown experienced over the past two decades is partly rooted in a rise of adjustment frictions that rein in the creative destruction process (Andrews et al., 2016; Gopinath, et al., 2015; Decker et al., 2016). One important dimension of this phenomenon is the growing share of firms that would typically exit or be forced to restructure in a competitive market (often referred to as "zombie firms") but manage to survive, to the detriment of aggregate productivity (Figure

3.1; Andrews et al. 2016). In this view, reviving productivity growth will, in part, depend on policies that effectively facilitate the exit or restructuring of weak firms.

Figure 3.1. The rise of zombie congestion[1]

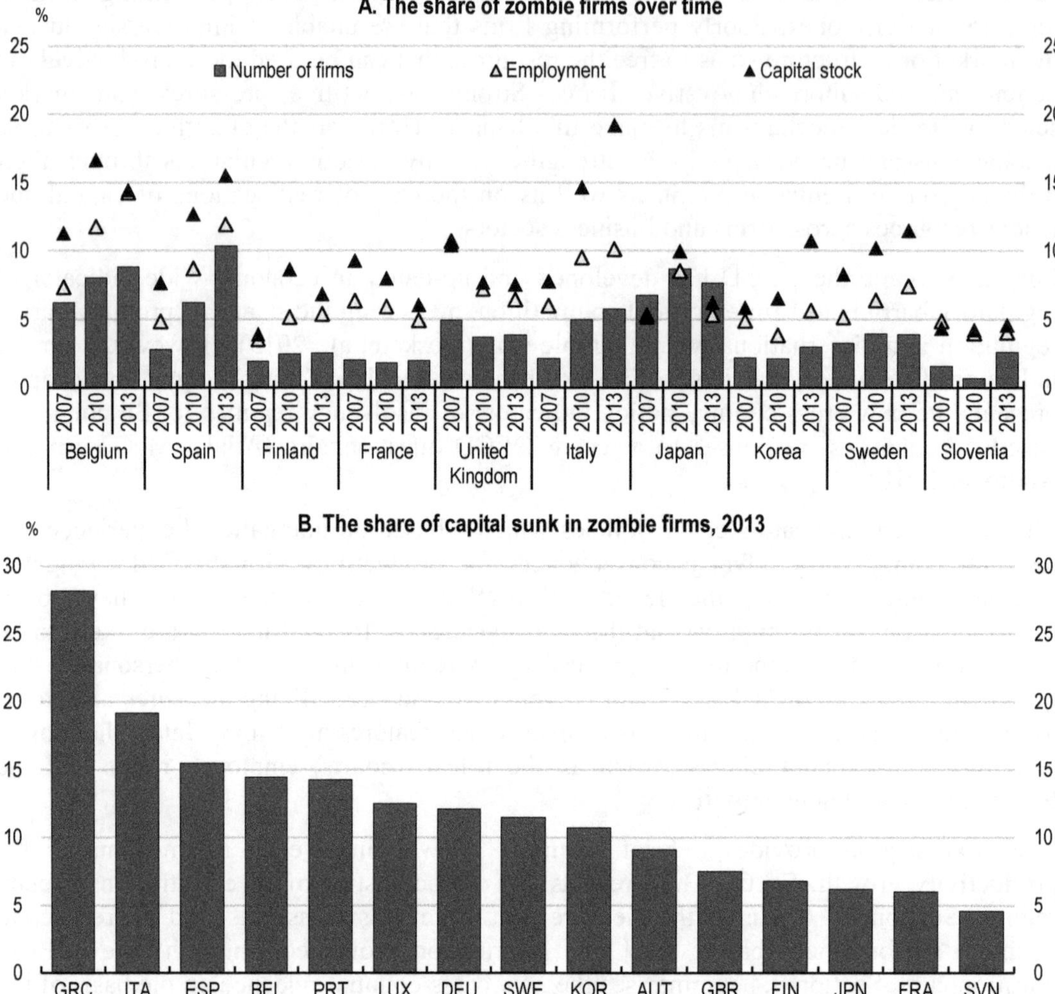

1. "Zombies" are defined as firms aged of 10 years and over, with an interest coverage ratio below 1 over three consecutive years.

Source: Adalet McGowan, M., D. Andrews and V. Millot (2017), "Insolvency regimes, zombie firms and capital reallocation", OECD Economics Department Working Papers, No. 1399, OECD Publishing.

StatLink http://dx.doi.org/10.1787/888933680419

3.3. The characteristics of effective insolvency regimes and how they can be assessed

The range of policies that affect exit and restructuring is broad. For instance, high barriers to entry can themselves constitute an obstacle to exit insofar as they allow low-performing firms to survive more easily, protecting them from stronger competition. Hence, regulations of product, labour and financial markets, as well as macroeconomic policies, government subsidies and guarantees, judicial efficiency and intellectual property regimes, taxation and vintage differentiated environmental regulation can all affect the strength of market selection and the scope and speed at which scarce resources employed by failing firms can be reallocated to more productive uses. Still, since market imperfections often generate obstacles to the orderly exit of failing firms, the efficiency of insolvency regimes emerges as particularly crucial among the many policies affecting the exit margin. One question is what are the basic characteristics of a well-functioning insolvency regime? This section discusses some of the features and briefly mentions existing measures.

3.3.1. General objectives of insolvency regimes

Market imperfections, such as coordination problems, incomplete contracts and information asymmetries, make it difficult in practice for the private market to facilitate the exit of failing firms in an orderly fashion. When a debtor is suspected of being insolvent, creditors have an incentive to engage in a "rush to the exit", rapidly enforcing their individual claims, even if it results in a reduction in the total value of recoverable assets or the chances of restructuring viable parts of the activity. In practice, it is also difficult for debtors and creditors to write a complete private contract that ensures an optimal outcome ex ante due to the high number of contingencies and the fact that the debtor can acquire new assets and liabilities after the initial contract (Hart, 2000). For these reasons, insolvency regimes that contain provisions to deal in an orderly fashion with the financial distress of commercial entities (i.e. corporate insolvency regimes) and entrepreneurs who have either been trading as a sole proprietor or who are part of a closely-held private company (i.e. personal insolvency regimes) are required.

Insolvency regimes need to balance an important trade-off: on the one hand, the incentives provided for investors to extend credit and to monitor firm performance, and on the other hand, the incentives provided to debtors to manage the firm efficiently and transparently. Insolvency regimes can promote efficient outcomes by providing these incentives: *i*) prior to insolvency when the firm is healthy (ex-ante efficiency); and *ii*) once the firm is in distress and enters insolvency (ex post efficiency). While ex ante efficiency will be important in order to discourage excessively risky behaviour from debtors and managers, currently available indicators – including the new indicators presented below – tend to place more emphasis on ex post efficiency incentives, partly because it is easier to measure. Moreover, while existing indicators focus on those design features that may impact the timely initiation and resolution of insolvency proceedings, the quality of resolution – which is very difficult to measure – will also matter.

Finally, while the objectives of insolvency regimes are well-established, there is less consensus on their optimal design. Given the complementarities between insolvency regimes and other institutional settings, there is no "one size fits all" approach. Nevertheless, a number of studies have outlined international best practices (IMF, 1999; INSOL, 2000; UNCITRAL, 2004; World Bank, 2015; Bricongne et al., 2016). A general lesson is that the regimes should be designed in a way to encourage debtors to take appropriate actions sufficiently early on in their financial difficulties, thereby increasing the chances of a successful restructuring.

3.3.2. Existing measures of insolvency regimes

One set of indicators of insolvency regimes available across countries is the World Bank Doing Business Indicators, which focuses on the cost in time and resources involved to go through insolvency procedures (Box 3.1). In doing so they cover both *de facto* and *de jure* aspects but put little direct emphasis on the numerous policy dimensions of insolvency regimes, making it difficult to identify their contribution to productivity performance and to generate country-specific proposals for policy reform – the task of *Going for Growth* (Adalet McGowan and Andrews, 2016).

In particular, the World Bank indicators focus primarily on corporate restructuring, whereas personal insolvency regimes are often more relevant for entrepreneurs and small businesses. Indeed, the corporate *vs* non-corporate distinction in assets and liabilities is often blurred for small firms, either because lenders require personal guarantees or security – e.g. a mortgage on the owner's home – or because prior to incorporating and obtaining limited liability protection, entrepreneurs typically use personal finances (Berkowitz and White, 2004; Cumming, 2012).[14]

Box 3.1. World Bank Doing Business Indicators – Resolving Insolvency

The World Bank Doing Business indicators include a Resolving Insolvency component with global coverage. The data for the resolving insolvency indicators are derived from questionnaire responses by local insolvency practitioners and the study of laws and regulations as well as public information on insolvency systems. The country rankings are based on performance with respect to two equally weighted sub-indicators:

- Outcome-based indicators: the recovery rate, based on the time, cost and outcome of insolvency proceedings based on a stylised case study.
- Strength of Insolvency Framework Index (introduced in 2015), based on four other indices: commencement of proceedings index, management of debtor's assets index, reorganization proceedings index and creditor participation index.

The use of a case study to derive the outcome based (*de facto*) indicators has both advantages and disadvantages. On the plus side, it is a direct attempt to gauge the average time and cost of insolvency proceedings given survey respondents typically find it difficult to give an exact answer to a general questionnaire without details on the complexity of the individual case. Moreover, being a *de facto* measure, it can capture the actual burdens of the insolvency regime, originating in institutions beyond the pure insolvency regime itself, such as an inefficient judicial system.

Yet, the case study comes at the cost of a loss of generality: referring only to corporate insolvency; involving only debt covered by collateral – i.e. the hotel, a tangible asset – while intangible assets are difficult to collateralise and can complicate the insolvency proceedings; relating only to one senior secured creditor, which is a bank, and not taking into account issues of priority, which is an important element of insolvency regimes; focusing only on formal insolvency proceedings as the respondents are not offered the option of out-of-court settlements and informal work-out options; and lacking the possibility of linking the outcomes directly to policies.

Source: http://www.doingbusiness.org/Methodology/Resolving-Insolvency

3.4. The new OECD indicators of insolvency regimes

To fill a gap and provide complementary insights,- in particular as regards to the identification of detailed policy-level reform needs, the OECD has designed and constructed a new set of indicators of insolvency regimes. The regulatory information used to compile the composite indicators has been collected through a questionnaire on corporate and personal insolvency regimes. The choice of questions and quantitative coding of the potential responses to each question are based on the main conclusions of the theoretical and empirical literature on the links between insolvency regimes and economic growth. The questionnaire was designed to capture design features of insolvency regimes in the following areas (Figure 3.2):

- *The treatment of failed entrepreneurs* – measuring the availability of a *fresh start* for failed entrepreneurs with respect to the time to discharge and exemptions of their personal assets from insolvency proceedings.
- *Prevention and streamlining* – summarising information on early warning mechanisms, pre-insolvency regimes and special simplified procedures for SMEs.
- *Tools related to actual restructuring*: the ability of creditors to initiate restructuring, the availability and length of stay on assets, the priority order of claimants (such as government or employees), the treatment ("cram-down") of dissenting creditors and the incumbent management.
- *Additional data* was collected on the role of courts, provisions distinguishing between honest and fraudulent bankruptcies and the rights of employees.

Figure 3.2. The structure of the OECD insolvency indicator[1]

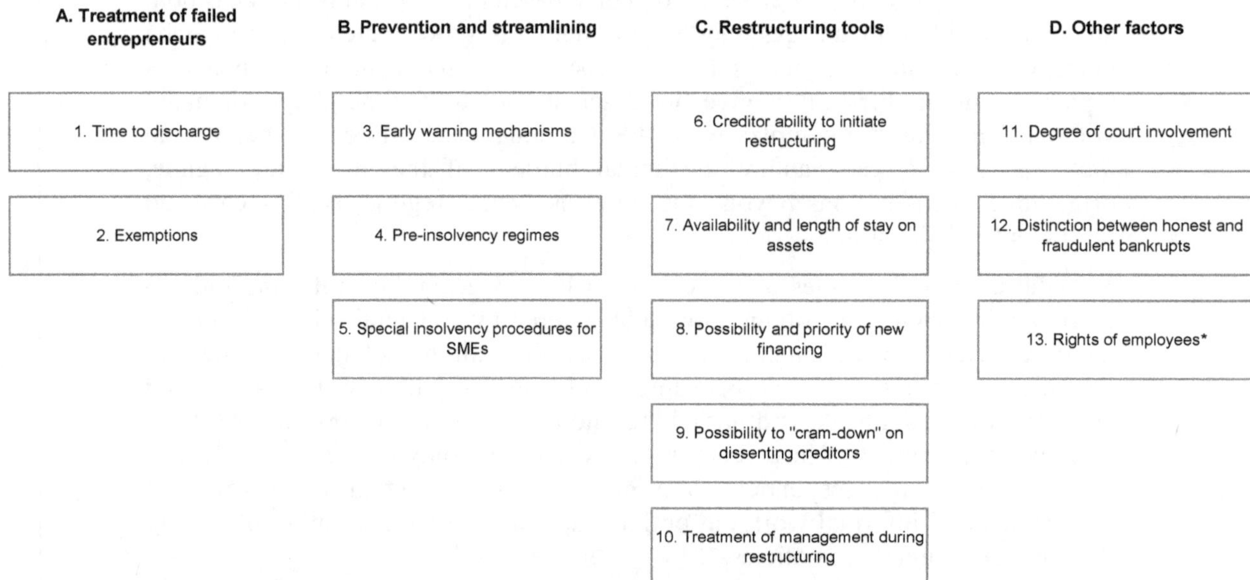

1. Data on Rights of Employees are missing for Denmark and Korea.
Source: Adalet McGowan, M., D. Andrews and V. Millot (2017), "Insolvency regimes, zombie firms and capital reallocation", OECD Economics Department Working Papers, No. 1399, OECD Publishing.

3.4.1. Treatment of failed entrepreneurs

A key dimension of personal insolvency regimes is the extent to which they "punish" failed entrepreneurs. Following the literature, the extent to which insolvency regimes limit entrepreneurs' ability to start new businesses following a failure will typically depend on: i) the availability of and the time to discharge (i.e. the number of years a bankrupt must wait until they are discharged from pre-bankruptcy indebtedness); ii) the extent of exemptions of assets of the debtor that are not directly linked to the business (e.g. the family house or a spouse's assets); and iii) the restrictions imposed on civil and economic rights of the debtor.[15]

Cross-country evidence suggests that lower personal costs to failed entrepreneurs can increase self-employment rates, small business owners' use of insolvency proceedings

(Armour and Cumming, 2008), firm entry rates (Lee, et al., 2007; Fan and White, 2003) and attract "better" entrepreneurs (Eberhart, 2014; Fossen, 2014). In particular, a lengthy time to discharge can discourage entrepreneurship by making it costlier to start risky businesses. The availability of a "fresh start" has been found to foster productivity growth via higher incentives for entrepreneurship and experimentation by: *i)* increasing firm entry (Cumming, 2012); *ii)* providing failed entrepreneurs with a second chance to apply their experience and lessons learnt to ensure their new businesses grow (Burchell and Hughes, 2006); and *iii)* attracting better quality entrepreneurs – i.e. individuals with higher observed human capital (Eberhart, et al., 2014).

However, facilitating a fresh start does not come without a trade-off. The literature suggests that full debt discharge after a limited period of time should be available for debtors, but the ideal length for the time to discharge is less straightforward. On one hand, a lengthy time to discharge can discourage entrepreneurship by making it costlier to start risky businesses. On the other hand, a short time to discharge can affect the behaviour of lenders and increase the cost of credit, which can adversely affect entrepreneurship. The exemptions of debtors' assets that are not directly linked to the business (e.g. the family house or a spouse's assets) have also a similar relationship to entrepreneurship and productivity as the time to discharge. For example, there is evidence that the generosity of exemptions can positively affect entrepreneurship by lowering the cost of failure and enabling more risk-averse individuals to start a business (Gropp et al., 1997), although they can also increase credit costs and collateral requirements (Berkowitz and White, 2004; Davydenko and Franks, 2008). At the same time, forced sale of assets can decrease their value of the proceeds that goes to the creditor (Campbell et al., 2011).

Against this backdrop, the OECD indicator assumes that a lengthier time to discharge is detrimental to productivity growth and hence is given a higher ("worse") value. Threshold values of one and three years are adopted for scoring, with the worst score given to a time to discharge above three years, in line with the 2016 proposal by the European Commission of the harmonisation of discharge periods in Europe to a maximum of three years for honest entrepreneurs. More generous exemptions are assumed less likely to delay the initiation of insolvency proceedings – hence are given a lower score in the indicator.

Looking at the indicator values, the personal costs to entrepreneurship are lowest in Canada, Turkey and the United States, while they are the highest in the Czech Republic (Figure 3.3). Reform activity in the area of personal costs to failed entrepreneurs has been limited, with only Chile, Greece and Spain undertaking reforms in this area between 2010 and 2016.

Figure 3.3. The availability of a fresh start

Stacked values of the low-level components of the treatment of failed entrepreneurs,[1] 2016

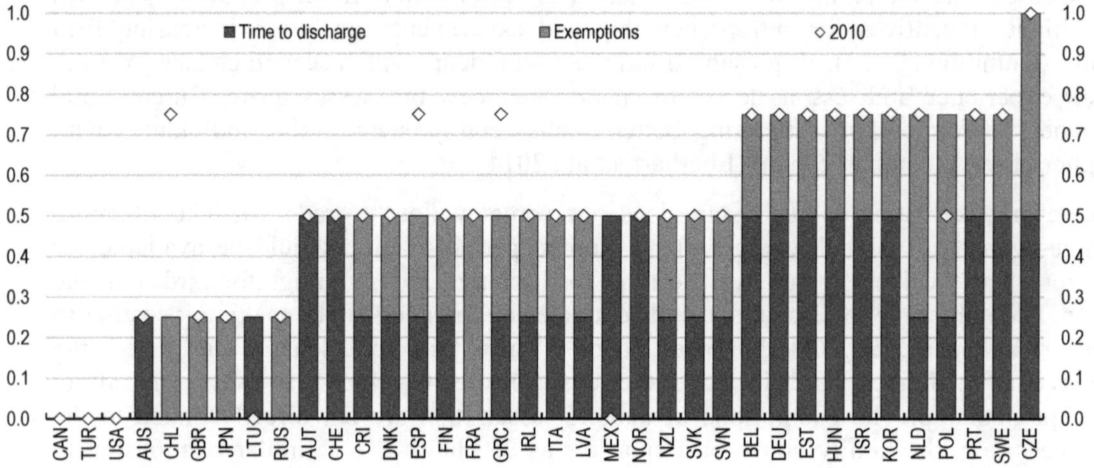

1. Time to discharge takes the value 0 if the time to discharge is less than or equal to one year, 0.5 if the time to discharge is between one and three years and 1 if the time to discharge is greater than three years (or is not available). Exemptions take the value 0 if exemptions (pre-bankruptcy assets which are exempt from the bankrupt estate) are more generous than modest personal items and working equipment (e.g. the debtor's house is exempt), 0.5 if exemptions are restricted to only modest personal items (e.g. assets or income required to cover the debtor's subsistence) and working equipment and 1 if exemptions are less generous. The sum is divided by 2 to range from 0 to 1.

Source: Adalet McGowan, A. and D. Andrews (2018), "Design of Insolvency Regimes across Countries", OECD Economics Department Working Papers, forthcoming.

StatLink http://dx.doi.org/10.1787/888933680438

There are significant cross-country differences in discharge possibilities. In fact, discharge is not available in Mexico, Norway and Switzerland. It is higher than three years in 10 other countries. Exemptions are most stringent in the Czech Republic, France, Poland and the Netherlands, where they are less generous than modest personal items and working equipment. The majority of countries in the sample limit exemptions to modest personal items and working equipment, while 9 countries have more generous exemptions.

3.4.2. Prevention and streamlining features

Early resolution of debt distress can maximise the value recovered for creditors and minimise the cost to the economy (Garrido, 2012). In practice, the lack of sufficient preventative and streamlining actions can be due to:

- A lack of early warning mechanisms and pre-insolvency regimes, which may push viable firms experiencing temporary financial distress into lengthy and costly formal insolvency proceedings, when firm distress could have been addressed via informal workouts (i.e. without the involvement of courts).
- An absence of special procedures for small and medium enterprises (SMEs), which could lead to many inefficient small firms continuing to operate because they lack scale to cover the fixed costs associated with formal insolvency proceedings.

Early warning tools, such as training offered to firms to assess their financial position and financial and debt counselling to companies with financial difficulties, and preventative restructuring frameworks such as pre-insolvency regimes are potentially important to the extent that they can assist the debtor in the assessment of the extent of risks involved, allow debtors and creditors to intervene early and if needed, negotiate informally before insolvency starts (Bricogne et al., 2016). The lack of or limited use of such measures, particularly in Southern European countries (Costantini, 2009), can push viable firms experiencing temporary financial distress into formal insolvency proceedings. Delays and higher costs associated with formal proceedings can erode the final value of the firm, prevent the quick reallocation of assets and resources of distressed firms to more productive uses and limit the opportunity of entrepreneurs to start a new business, lowering business dynamism.

Small and medium enterprises (SMEs) may warrant a different treatment from other firms in a debt restructuring strategy as complex, lengthy and rigid procedures, as well as required expertise and high costs of insolvency can fail to adequately meet the needs of SMEs (EC, 2011; 2013). Furthermore, some SMEs are owned and operated by families who have pledged their personal assets for loans. As a result, business insolvency may lead to personal insolvency once a business fails, even where the business is a separate legal entity (Bergthaler et al., 2015). Hence, special insolvency procedures for SMEs – such as simplified or pre-packaged in-court proceedings targeting SMEs or the possibility to have instalments in the payment of administrative expenses related to the insolvency proceedings – could ensure that non-viable ones exit and viable ones in temporary distress are restructured without delay. Clearly, such measures need to be assessed with caution, as the policy discontinuity may add a barrier to SME growth – however, in case of insolvency procedures this is not likely to be a major issue.

The indicator counts the existence of early warning mechanisms, pre-insolvency regimes and special insolvency procedures for SMEs, with a score of zero translating into full prevalence of prevention and streamlining features across the three fields, i.e. the country has at least one procedure in place in all of them.

Early-warning mechanisms are present in only one-third of the countries analysed, suggesting that there is ample room for reform in this area (Figure 3.4). Pre-insolvency regimes tend to be in place in many European countries, but they are notably lacking in the Czech Republic, Estonia, Finland, Hungary, Lithuania, the Slovak Republic and Sweden. Moreover, they are not widespread in non-European OECD countries such as Australia, Canada, Mexico and the United States. In total, 25 countries do not have special insolvency procedures for SMEs, which could lead to many inefficient small firms continuing to operate because they lack scale to cover the fixed costs associated with formal insolvency proceedings. Over time, insolvency reform efforts have been more important and widespread in the area of prevention and streamlining between 2010 and 2016, especially in European countries, with reforms observable in 11 countries.

Figure 3.4. Features to enable early detection and resolution of debt distress

Stacked low-level components of prevention and streamlining,[1] 2016

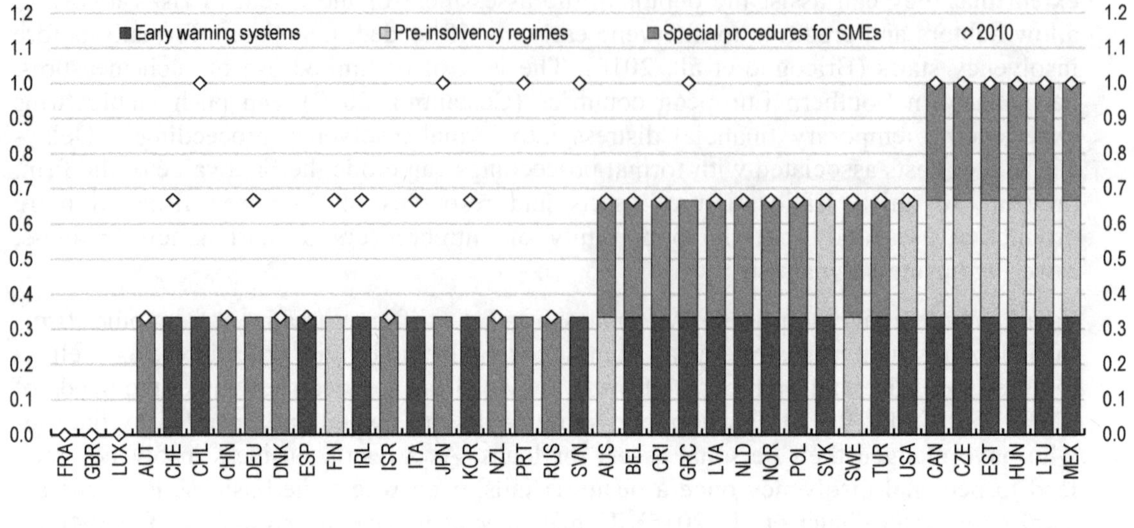

1. Early warning systems are equal to 0 if countries have early warning mechanisms (e.g. on-line self-test, training) in place and 1 otherwise. Pre-insolvency regimes are equal to 0 if pre-insolvency regimes exist and 1 otherwise. Special procedures for SMEs take the value 0 if special insolvency procedures exist for SMEs and 1 otherwise. The sum is divided by 3 to range from 0 to 1.

Source: Adalet McGowan, A. and D. Andrews (2018), "Design of Insolvency Regimes across Countries", OECD Economics Department Working Papers, forthcoming.

StatLink http://dx.doi.org/10.1787/888933680457

3.4.3. Restructuring tools

Design features of corporate insolvency regimes should support the rehabilitation of viable firms (Djankov et al., 2008) by lowering the barriers to restructuring. The chances of success of a restructuring process can be increased by design features that promote the timely initiation of restructuring and the continuity of firm operations. Such design features include:

- *Creditors are able to initiate restructuring.* The possibility of starting restructuring procedures early is a key element of an efficient insolvency regime as delays can increase costs and reduce the likelihood of a successful restructuring (World Bank, 2015; Bricongne et al., 2016). As a result, non-viable firms are less likely to linger in the market and viable firms which encounter temporary financial distress are less likely to become impaired due to a lack of impetus to restructure. As the debtor may have incentives to delay restructuring, it is crucial to give the creditor the opportunity and the right incentives to initiate such procedures.
- *A stay on assets is possible.*[16] The continuity of firm operations during the restructuring process increases the chances of a successful restructuring. A stay on assets provides room for parties to negotiate without the interruption of enforcement actions, while the absence of a stay on assets can lead to premature liquidations, even when the value of keeping the firm in operation is higher than its liquidation value (Wruck, 1990). This can increase the probability of viable firms being liquidated, but also discourage entrepreneurs from starting a new

business in the first place and affect the innovation strategies adopted by entrants. On the other hand, if creditors have limited ability to recuperate their loan, this can increase the cost of credit, which can adversely affect entrepreneurship (Armour and Cumming, 2008; Lee et al., 2011; Broadie et al., 2007). Hence, safeguards are necessary to ensure that the stay is time-limited and be used strictly to facilitate a restructuring plan.

- *There is the possibility of priority ("seniority") available to new financing over unsecured creditors.* Priority rules, which refer to the order in which various stakeholders get paid in the event of liquidation, are specified ex ante in the debt contract in accordance with general insolvency laws, but there might be ex post deviations from absolute priority rules. Typically, senior creditors are paid in full prior to any payment being made to junior creditors and the detailed priority rights of securitised creditors, employees, suppliers and tax authorities vary across countries. Retaining the (ex-ante) priority order increases the efficiency of the system by making it more predictable and fair. However, deviations from absolute priority may be warranted (e.g. priority for new financing), when it might lead to a successful restructuring and a higher final recovery value for all creditors (EC 2014a and 2014b; Bergthaler et al., 2015). The extent and the exact design of the priority is less clear cut. International best practice suggests that such new financing should be granted priority ahead of unsecured creditors. However, it is important to ensure that existing creditors do not exploit the priority of new financing to move on to the top of the queue, by injecting new capital to the firm. Unless it is agreed by the secured creditors, post-commencement financing should normally not have priority over existing secured creditors since this would adversely affect the availability of credit and legal certainty.[17]
- *It is possible to "cram-down" on dissenting creditors that try to block a restructuring plan.*[18] Requiring a unanimous vote by all creditors on a restructuring plan can delay proceedings. Thus, allowing the approval of such a plan by only a requisite majority of creditors (the so-called "cram-down") can strengthen market selection by promoting the timely restructuring of viable firms that encounter temporary financial difficulties, and deliver higher future within-firm productivity gains (Bricongne et al., 2016). Again, in order to prevent the potential adverse effects on credit supply, it is important that the interests of dissenting creditors are protected by ensuring that they are treated equally to other creditors within the same class and would receive under the plan at least as much as they would receive under liquidation.
- *Incumbent management is not automatically dismissed during restructuring.* Allowing incumbent managers to stay in charge of the day-to-day operations of a firm in distress rather than forcing them out during restructuring proceedings can affect productivity in conflicting ways. Insolvency regimes that do not provide sufficient cover for incumbent management increase the private incentives of management to hide the true financial state of the firm and gamble on resurrection (Marinč and Vlahu, 2012). This would likely weaken market selection and, by delaying the process, reduce the chance that restructuring is successful in delivering higher future productivity gains. These channels will also operate if the retention of incumbent management increases the incentives for management to make firm-specific productivity-enhancing investments in the event that new financing is available (von Thadden et al., 2010; Ayotte, 2007).[19] Against this, retaining incumbent management could weaken market selection if it incentivises secured creditors to liquidate, rather than restructure, viable firms (Kaiser,

1996).[20] Despite these trade-offs, it is assumed that dismissal of management during restructuring can have largely adverse effect on the timely initiation of insolvency.

For each of the aforementioned areas, the indicator takes the value of zero for no impediments to restructuring (i.e. creditors are able to initiate restructuring, a limited stay on assets is possible, cram-down with certain conditions is possible new financing has seniority over unsecured creditors, management is not automatically fired). In 14 countries (Figure 3.5), only debtors can initiate restructuring. A stay on assets during restructuring is available in all countries, but the length of the stay varies and around half of the countries analysed has an indefinite length of stay on assets during restructuring. There are significant cross-country differences both in terms of the availability and the priority of new financing to distressed or restructuring firms. Priority only over unsecured creditors is possible for new financing in 20 countries. New financing can have priority over both secured and unsecured creditors in 11 countries, while in the remaining 6 countries there is no priority for new financing.

Figure 3.5. Barriers to restructuring

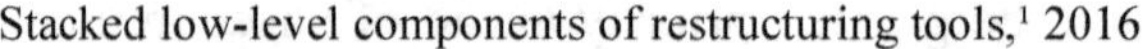

Stacked low-level components of restructuring tools,[1] 2016

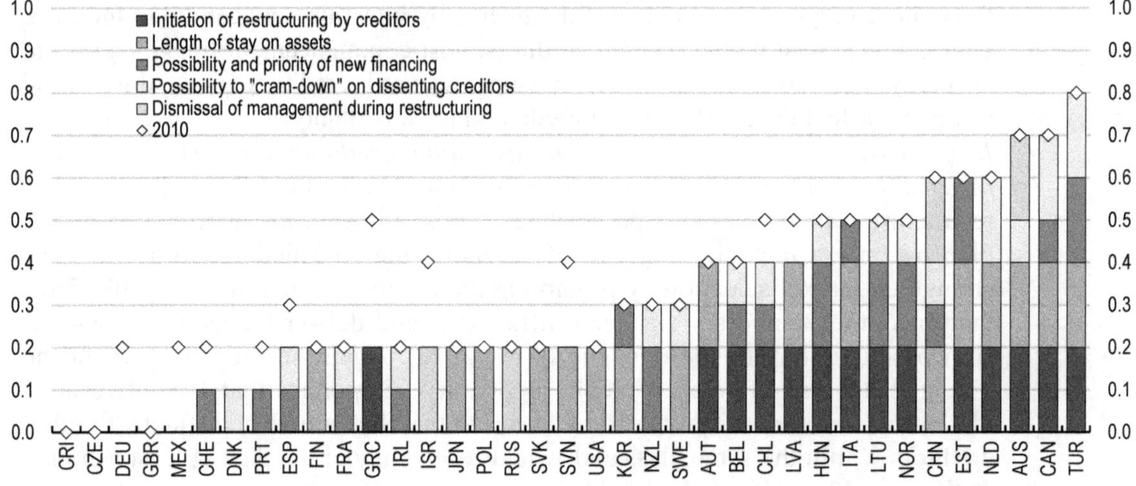

1. Initiation of restructuring by creditors is equal to 0 if creditors can initiate both liquidation and restructuring and 1 if creditors can initiate only liquidation. Length of stay on assets in restructuring is equal to 0 if the length of stay has a limit and 1 if the length of stay is indefinite. Possibility and priority of new financing is equal to 0 if the new financing has priority over only unsecured creditors, 0.5 if the priority of new financing has priority over both secured and unsecured creditors and 1 if new financing has no priority. Possibility to cram-down on dissenting creditors is equal to 0 if there is cram-down, with the provision that dissenting creditors receive as much under restructuring as in liquidation, 0.5 if cram-down exists in the absence of this provision and 1 if there is no cram-down. Dismissal of management during restructuring is equal to 0 if management is not dismissed during the restructuring process and 1 if management is dismissed. The sum is divided by 5 to range from 0 to 1.

Source: Adalet McGowan, A. and D. Andrews (2018), "Design of Insolvency Regimes across Countries", OECD Economics Department Working Papers, forthcoming.

StatLink http://dx.doi.org/10.1787/888933680476

The possibility of cram-down on dissenting creditors is absent in only in three countries – Canada, the Netherlands and Turkey. Among the countries where cram-down is possible,

13 do not have the provision that dissenting creditors should receive at least as much under the restructuring plan as they would receive under liquidation – leaving room to reform towards best practice. Management does not necessarily get dismissed in all but four countries, namely Australia, China, Israel and the Russian Federation. Overall, barriers to restructuring have declined in 10 countries between 2010 and 2016.

3.4.4. Other design features

Finally, the indicator also surveyed three *additional* factors:

- *A high degree of court involvement, which may prolong the exit or restructuring of weak firms*, particularly in countries with inefficient judicial systems. Court involvement – directly or through court-appointed insolvency practitioners – is important in guaranteeing the rights of different parties involved and can increase ex post efficiency by acting as a coordination tool. However, court involvement can come at a cost – particularly for smaller firms that lack scale to cover the associated fixed costs (Bergthaler et al., 2015). Although some stages of a restructuring process require court involvement, most procedural steps – in principle and in relatively straightforward cases – can be dealt with out-of-court. Doing so could reduce the workload of the courts, enabling them to focus on a more timely resolution of those difficult cases where court involvement is necessary (Franks and Sussman, 2001; Betker, 1997). Limiting the involvement of courts to where it is only necessary can raise aggregate productivity by facilitating the exit of non-viable firms (i.e. strengthening market selection) and release scarce resources to be re-deployed to more productive uses. The indicator has been based on the number of different stages of insolvency proceedings (for both restructuring and liquidation) where courts are involved (up to 5, rescaled to be between 0 and 1). It remains a proxy as there are large complementarities between this feature and judicial efficiency (Ponticelli, 2015).
- *Stringent restrictions on worker dismissals and collective dismissals that cannot be negotiated during proceedings,* which may delay the exit or downsizing of weak firms. Obviously, the goal of restrictions on dismissals is not to impede firm exit or restructuring, but as a side effect, such restrictions can create a bias away from liquidation of non-viable firms, which can adversely affect productivity.[21] The indicator takes a value of 0 if there are no restrictions on the ability to dismiss employees upon the initiation of insolvency proceedings and it is possible to renegotiate collective dismissal agreements with employees. It takes the value of 0.5 if there are no restrictions on the ability to dismiss employees upon the initiation of insolvency proceedings but it is not possible to renegotiate collective dismissal agreements with employees or if there are restrictions on the ability to dismiss employees upon the initiation of insolvency proceedings but it is possible to renegotiate collective dismissal agreements with employees; and 1 if there are restrictions on the ability to dismiss employees upon the initiation of insolvency proceedings and it is not possible to renegotiate collective dismissal agreements with employees.
- *An insufficient distinction between honest and fraudulent bankrupts,* which raises the costs and the stigma of failure of insolvency proceedings, making it less likely that weak firms exit the market in a timely fashion. The indicator takes the value 0 if there is a distinction between the treatment of honest and fraudulent entrepreneurs in the insolvency process (e.g. a fraudulent entrepreneur may be ineligible for debt write-off or discharge from debt) and 1 otherwise.

The degree of court involvement in liquidation and restructuring is lowest in Korea and highest in Canada, Costa Rica, Austria and Slovenia (Figure 3.6). Similarly, there are significant cross-country differences in terms of employee rights during liquidation and restructuring, with the most stringent restrictions in Austria, Slovenia and the Slovak Republic. Finally, the differentiation in the treatment of honest and fraudulent entrepreneurs, which is crucial for an effective second chance, is available in 29 out of the countries analysed.

Figure 3.6. Other design features

Stacked low-level components of other factors,[1] 2016

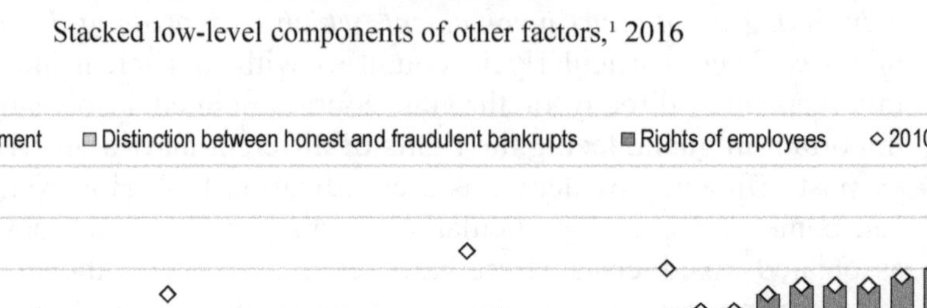

1. Degree of court involvement adds the number of stages in which courts are involved for restructuring (from 0 to 5) and number of stages for liquidation (from 0 to 5), and is then rescaled between 0 and 1. Distinction between honest and fraudulent bankrupts takes the value 0 if there is a distinction between the treatment of honest and fraudulent entrepreneurs in the insolvency process and 1 otherwise. For both liquidation and restructuring the indicator is defined as equal to 0 if there are no restrictions on the ability to dismiss employees upon the initiation of insolvency proceedings and it is possible to renegotiate collective dismissal agreements with employees; 1 if there are no restrictions on the ability to dismiss employees upon the initiation of insolvency proceedings but it is not possible to renegotiate collective dismissal agreements with employees or if there are restrictions on the ability to dismiss employees upon the initiation of insolvency proceedings but it is possible to renegotiate collective dismissal agreements with employees; and 2 if there are restrictions on the ability to dismiss employees upon the initiation of insolvency proceedings and it is not possible to renegotiate collective dismissal agreements with employees. The two are summed and rescaled to be between 0 and 1. The sum is divided by 3 to range from 0 to 1.

Source: Adalet McGowan, A. and D. Andrews (2018), "Design of Insolvency Regimes across Countries", OECD Economics Department Working Papers, forthcoming.

StatLink http://dx.doi.org/10.1787/888933680495

3.5. Cross-country differences in overall insolvency regimes

The data on the various OECD sub-indicators has been combined in a composite insolvency regime indicator through a bottom-up approach, allowing tracing indicator scores back to individual policies. The aggregation applies equal weights to each of them, where each of the four main dimensions (Figure 3.4) have been all rescaled in order to have the aggregate indicator on insolvency regimes ranging between 0 and 1 – with 1 signalling the highest impediments to a smooth exit or successful restructuring (Figure 3.7).

According to these combined metrics, cross-country differences in the design of insolvency regimes are significant. For example, the United Kingdom's low value reflects the fact that the personal costs associated with entrepreneurial failure and barriers to restructuring are low, while there is also a number of provisions to aid prevention and streamlining. On the contrary, the high value for Estonia comes from an almost equal contribution of the three subcomponents.[22]

Figure 3.7. Composite indicator of insolvency regimes

Scale of 0 to 1 from least to most stringent

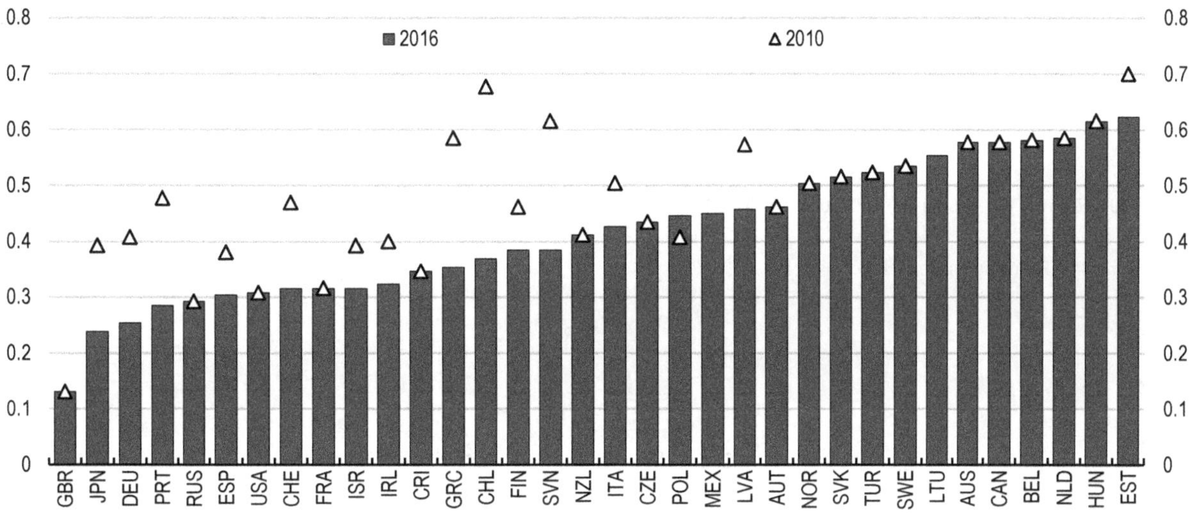

Source: Adalet McGowan, A. and D. Andrews (2018), "Design of Insolvency Regimes across Countries", OECD Economics Department Working Papers, forthcoming.

StatLink http://dx.doi.org/10.1787/888933680514

Along with Estonia, Australia, Italy, Poland and Portugal are the OECD countries for which a priority has been identified in this area in the last edition of Going for Growth (OECD, 2017). Most are in the top half of the distribution depicted by the aggregate insolvency indicator and perform mid-rank on the World Bank's Doing Business Resolving Insolvency indicator (Figure 3.8). Interestingly, Estonia, Portugal, Poland and Italy tend to rank somewhat better on the *de jure* WB Strength of Insolvency Framework index than on the de facto WB Recovery Rate.

Across time, a comparison of the 2010 and 2016 values for the three sub-indicators shows that 15 countries have reformed their insolvency regimes recently. The countries with the biggest reform in this area are Chile, Germany, Greece, Japan, Portugal and Slovenia. The reform efforts have concentrated on prevention and streamlining, with reforms observable in 11 countries, especially European countries (e.g. Portugal). This may partly reflect the fact that such measures have been recently endorsed by the European Commission and the IMF, in response to the crisis (Carcea et al., 2015; Bergthaler et al., 2015). Barriers to restructuring have also declined in 10 countries, while reform activity affecting the personal costs to failed entrepreneurs has been less ambitious, with only Chile, Greece and Spain undertaking reforms since 2010. Notably, of the set of countries with a *Going for Growth* priority on insolvency regimes, significant reforms have taken place between 2010 and 2016 but only in Southern Europe: Portugal and Italy. As reported in Chapter 1, reforms have continued in Italy in 2017.

Figure 3.8. The OECD and World Bank insolvency indicators[1]

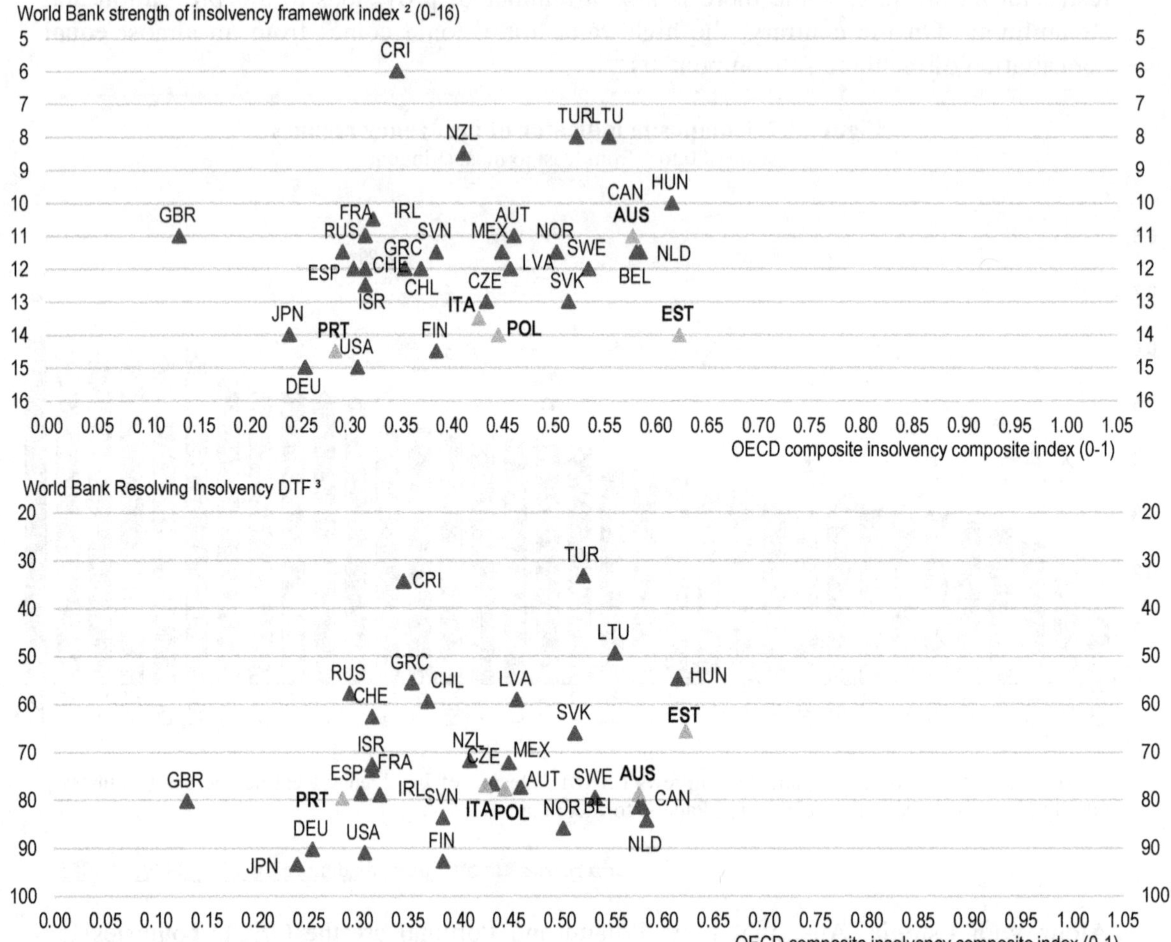

1. Red marker and bold labels indicates countries with a 2017 *Going for Growth* recommendation on insolvency regimes.
2. The World Bank strength of insolvency framework index is based on four other indices: commencement of proceedings index, management of debtor's assets index, reorganization proceedings index and creditor participation index. The strength of insolvency framework index is the sum of the scores on the commencement of proceedings index, management of debtor's assets index, reorganization proceedings index and creditor participation index. The index ranges from 0 to 16, with higher values indicating insolvency legislation that is better designed for rehabilitating viable firms and liquidating nonviable ones.
3. The data for the resolving insolvency indicators are derived from questionnaire responses by local insolvency practitioners and verified through a study of laws and regulations as well as public information on insolvency systems. The ranking of economies on the ease of resolving insolvency is determined by sorting their distance to frontier scores for resolving insolvency.
Source: Adalet McGowan, A. and D. Andrews (2018), "Design of Insolvency Regimes across Countries", OECD Economics Department Working Papers, forthcoming; World Bank, Doing Business.

StatLink http://dx.doi.org/10.1787/888933680533

The new OECD insolvency indicators constitute an important tool to assess the impact of insolvency regimes on economic performance and will allow for a better integration in *Going for Growth* of the exit margin to set countries' priorities. For example, recent research using the new indicators shows that reforms to insolvency regimes can: i) reduce the share of capital sunk in zombie firms, which in turn spurs the reallocation of capital to more productive firms (Adalet McGowan, Andrews and Millot, 2017a, Figure 3.9); and ii) facilitate technological diffusion by promoting experimentation and providing laggard firms with the scope to implement the necessary business changes to move closer to the technological frontier (Adalet McGowan, Andrews and Millot, 2017b). The indicators also allow for cross-country comparisons of certain design features of insolvency regimes and the monitoring of over time changes, providing key information for the conduct of OECD country reviews of economic performance and structural policy reforms.

Figure 3.9. Simulated gains in aggregate labour productivity from the reduction of zombie congestion[1]

2013

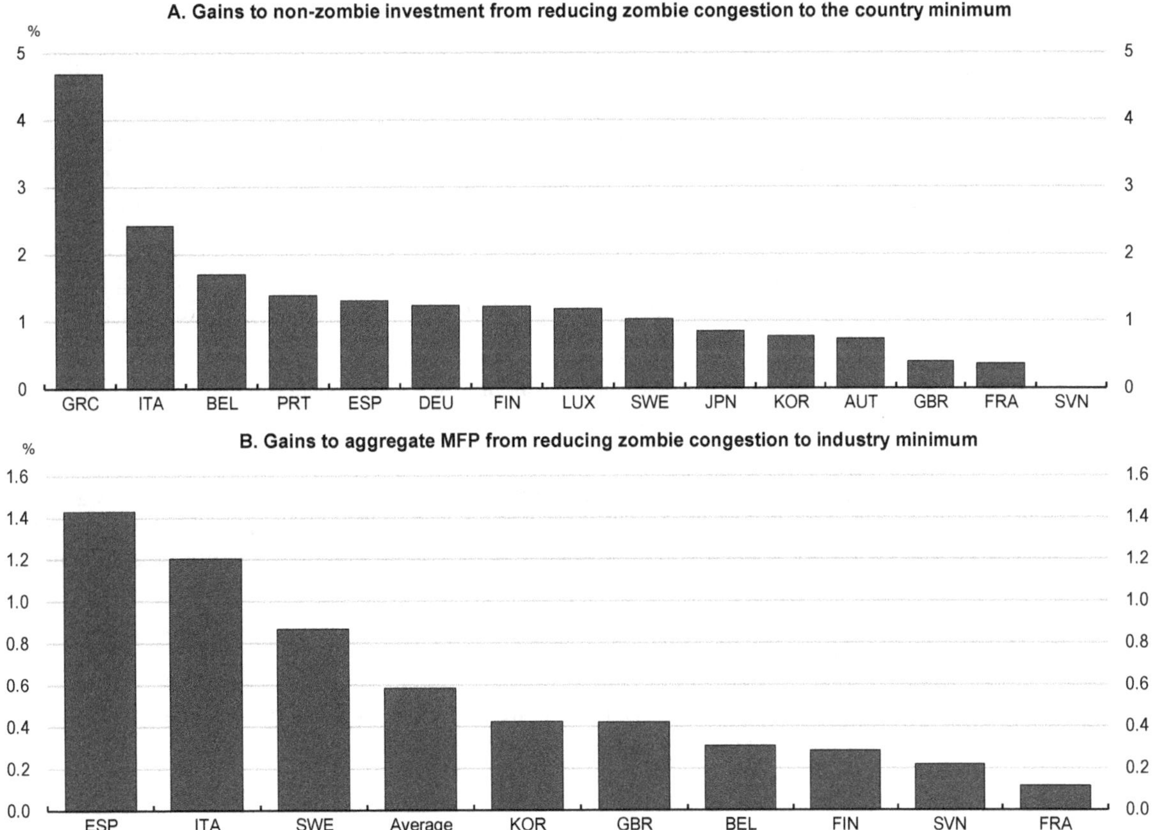

1. Zombie firms are defined as firms aged of 10 years and over, with an interest coverage ratio below 1 over three consecutive years. Panel A shows the simulated gains to investment of a typical non-zombie firm from reducing the share of zombies to the sample minimum level (i.e. Slovenia in 2013). Panel B shows the simulated gains to aggregate business sector MFP via more efficient capital reallocation from reducing the shares of zombies in each country to the sample minimum level in each industry and year. The country level numbers are an unweighted average of all industries (2-digit level detail according to NACE Rev. 2, covering the non-farm non-financial business sector).

Source: Adalet McGowan, M., D. Andrews and V. Millot (2017), "Insolvency regimes, zombie firms and capital reallocation", OECD Economics Department Working Papers, No. 1399, OECD Publishing.

StatLink http://dx.doi.org/10.1787/888933680552

Endnotes

13. Environmentally related taxes are defined as any compulsory, unrequited payment to government levied specifically on tax bases deemed to be of environmental relevance, i.e. taxes that have a tax base with a proven, specific negative impact on the environment, such as: energy products, transport equipment and services, pollution and natural resources. The definition includes revenues from auctioning of emission permits. Environmentally related taxes increase the costs of a polluting product or activity, which tends to discourage its production or consumption, regardless of what was the intention behind the introduction of the tax.

14. WB indicators also do not fully capture the availability and the length of the stay on assets, the fate of management and prevention and streamlining tools as they only focus on formal insolvency proceedings. In principle, some of these gaps can be addressed using the data from the European Commission (Carcea et al., 2015) – including the role of courts and the fate of incumbent management –, but the coverage is limited to- a sub-sample of European countries in 2012.

15. These include: *i)* the loss of power to deal with assets; loss of the right to vote or hold elected office; *ii)* restrictions on obtaining credit or on being involved in the management of a firm; and *iii)* restrictions on travel or interception of mail or being incarcerated for non-payment of debt.

16. A stay on assets stops actions by creditors, with certain exceptions, to collect debts from a debtor.

17. This applies to cases when all creditors still are more likely to recover their investment with a successful restructuring than in the alternative case of liquidation. Secured creditors refer to those lenders which hold a secured claim, i.e. secured by collateral taken as a guarantee to enforce a debt in case of the debtor's default.

18. The indicator also takes into account design features that ensure that dissenting creditors receive as much under the restructuring plan as they would in the case of liquidation (which is likely to lead to more restructuring).

19. The design of management compensation schemes will also affect incentives for firms to undertake costly productivity-enhancing investments, where the benefits might only be realised with a lag.

20. Furthermore, allowing management to stay on the job can be perceived by creditors as a block to secure repayment on their debt, thereby increasing the cost of credit and reducing firm entry rates, especially if creditors believe that managers can default strategically (Moulton and Thomas, 1993).

21. There is a question of whether there are more efficient tools to support workers displaced by firm exit – such as active labour market policies (Andrews and Saia, 2016).

22. Note that the number of countries can differ across sub-indicators, depending on responses received. The aggregation is hence possible for 34 countries only.

References

Adalet McGowan, M. and D. Andrews (2016), "Insolvency Regimes and Productivity Growth: A Framework for Analysis", OECD Economics Department Working Papers, No. 1309.

Adalet McGowan, M. and D. Andrews (2015), "Skill Mismatch and Public Policy in OECD countries", OECD Economics Department Working Paper, No. 1210.

Adalet McGowan, M. and D. Andrews (2018), "Design of Insolvency Regimes across Countries", OECD Economics Department Working Papers, forthcoming, OECD Publishing, Paris.

Adalet McGowan, M., D. Andrews and V. Millot (2017a), "Insolvency Regimes, Zombie Firms and Capital Reallocation", OECD Economics Department Working Papers, No. 1399.

Adalet McGowan, M., D. Andrews and V. Millot (2017b), "Insolvency Regimes, Technology Diffusion and Productivity Growth: Evidence from Firms in OECD Countries", OECD Economics Department Working Papers, No. 1425.

Andrews, D., C. Criscuolo and C. Menon (2014), "Do Resources Flow to Patenting Firms?: Cross-Country Evidence from Firm Level Data", OECD Economics Department Working Papers, No. 1127.

Andrews, D. and F. Cingano (2014), "Public Policy and Resource Allocation: Evidence from Firms in OECD Countries", Economic Policy, No. 29(78), pp. 253-296.

Andrews, D. and A. Saia (2016), "Coping with Creative Destruction: Reducing the Costs of Firm Exit", OECD Economics Department Working Papers, No. 1353.

Andrews, D. and F. Petroulakis (2017), "Breaking the Shackles: Zombie Firms, Weak Banks and Depressed Restructuring in Europe", OECD Economics Department Working Papers, No. 1433.

Armour, J. and D. Cumming (2006), "The Legislative Road to Silicon Valley", Oxford Economic Papers, Vol. 58.

Armour, J. and D. Cumming (2008), "Bankruptcy Law and Entrepreneurship", American Law Economic Review, Vol. 10, No. 2.

Ayotte, K. (2007), "Bankruptcy and Entrepreneurship: The Value of a Fresh Start", Journal of Law, Economics and Organisation, Vol. 23.

Bergthaler, W., K. Kang, Y. Liu and D. Monaghan (2015), "Tackling Small and Medium-sized Enterprise Problem Loans in Europe", IMF Staff Discussion Note, No. 4.

Berkowitz, J. and M. White (2004), "Bankruptcy and Small Firms' Access to Credit", RAND Journal of Economics, Vol. 35.

Betker, B. (1997), "The Administrative Costs of Debt Restructurings: Some Recent Evidence", Financial Management, Vol. 26.

Bouis, R., R. Duval and J. Eugster (2016), "Product Market Deregulation and Growth: New Country-Industry-Level Evidence", IMF Working Paper, WP/16/114.

Bricogne, J.C., M. Demertzis, P. Pontuch and A. Turrini (2016), "Macroeconomic Relevance of Insolvency Frameworks in a High-debt Context: An EU Perspective", European Commission Discussion Papers, No. 32.

Burchell, B. and A. Hughes (2006), "The Stigma of Failure: An International Comparison of Failure Tolerance and Second Chancing", University of Cambridge Centre for Business Research Working Papers, No. 334.

Campbell, Y.J., S. Giglio and P. Pathak (2011), "Forced Sales and House Prices", American Economic Review, Vol. 101, No. 5.

Carcea, M.C., D. Ciriraci, C. Cuerpo, D. Lorenzani and P. Pontuch (2015), "The Economic Impact of Rescue and Recovery Frameworks in the EU", European Commission Discussion Papers, No. 4.

Costantini, J. (2009), "Effects of Bankruptcy Procedures on Firm Restructuring: Evidence from Italy", mimeo.

Cumming, D. (2012), "Measuring the Effect of Bankruptcy Laws on Entrepreneurship across Countries", Journal of Entrepreneurial Finance, Vol. 16.

Davydenko, S. and J. Franks (2008), "Do Bankruptcy Codes Matter? A Study of Defaults in France, Germany and the UK", The Journal of Finance, Vol. 63, No.2.

Decker, R., J. Haltiwanger, R. Jarmin and J. Miranda (2016), "Changing Business Dynamism: Volatility of Shocks vs. Responsiveness to Shocks", mimeo.

Djankov, S., O. Hart, C. McLiesh and A. Shleifer (2008), "Debt Enforcement Around the World", Journal of Political Economy, Vol. 116, No. 6.

Eberhart, R., C. Eesley and K. Eisenhardt (2014), "Failure is an Option: Failure Barriers and New Firm Performance", Rock Centre for Corporate Governance at Stanford University Working Paper, No. 111.

European Commission (2014a), Impact Assessment: Commission Recommendation on a New Approach to Business Failure and Insolvency, Brussels.

European Commission (2014b), Commission Recommendation on a New Approach to Business Failure and Insolvency, Brussels.

Fan, W. and M. White (2003), ""Personal Bankruptcy and the Level of Entrepreneurial Activity", Journal of Law and Economics, Vol. 46.

Fossen, F. (2014), "Personal Bankruptcy Law, Wealth, and Entrepreneurship—Evidence from the Introduction of a Fresh Start Policy", American Law and Economics Review, Vol. 16.

Franks, J. and O. Sussman (2001), "Resolving Financial Distress by Way of a Contract: An Empirical Study of Small UK Companies", mimeo.

Garrido, J. (2012), Out-of Court Debt Restructuring, World Bank, Washington, DC.

Gopinath, G., S. Kalemli-Ozcan, L. Karabarbounis and C. Villegas-Sanchez (2015), "Capital Allocation and Productivity in South Europe", NBER Working Paper, No. 21453.

Gropp, R., J. Scholz and M. White (1997), "Personal Bankruptcy and Credit Supply and Demand", The Quarterly Journal of Economics, Vol. 112Hart, O. (2000), "Different Approaches to Bankruptcy", NBER Working Paper Series, No. 7921.

Hart, O. (2000), "Different Approaches to Bankruptcy", NBER Working Paper Series, No. 7921.

IMF (1999), Orderly and Effective Insolvency Procedures, Washington, DC.

International Federation of Insolvency Professionals-- INSOL (2000), Statement of Principles for a Global Approach to Multi-Creditor Workouts, London.

Koske, I., I. Wanner, R. Bitetti and O. Barbiero (2015), "The 2013 Update of the OECD's Database on Product Market Regulation: Policy Insights for OECD and non-OECD Countries", OECD Economics Department Working Papers, No. 1200.

Laryea, T. (2010), "Approaches to Corporate Debt Restructuring in the Wake of The Financial Crisis", IMF Staff Position Note, No. 02.

Lee, S., Y. Yamakawa, M. Peng, J. Barney (2011), "How do Bankruptcy Laws Affect Entrepreneurship Development Around the World?", Journal of Business Venturing, Vol. 26.

Lee, S., M. Peng and J. Barney (2007), "Bankruptcy Law and Entrepreneurship Development: A Real Options Perspective", Academy of Management Review, Vol. 32, No. 1.

Marinc, M. and R. Vlahu (2012), The Economics of Bank Bankruptcy Law, Springer-Verlag, Berlin Heidelberg.

Moulton, W. and T. Howard (1993), "Bankruptcy as a Deliberate Strategy: Theoretical Considerations and Empirical Evidence", Strategic Management Journal, Vol. 14.

Quinn, J. (1985), "Corporate Reorganization and Strategic Behaviour: An Economic Analysis of Canadian Insolvency Law and Recent Proposals for Reform", Osgoode Hall Law Journal, Vol. 23.

Ponticelli, J. (2015), "Court Enforcement, Bank Loans and Firm Investment: Evidence from a Bankruptcy Reform in Brazil", Chicago Booth Research Paper, No. 14-08.

Saia, A., D. Andrews and S. Albrizio (2015), "Productivity Spillovers from the Global Frontier and Public Policy: Industry Level Evidence", OECD Economics Department Working Paper, No. 1238.

United Nations Commission on International Trade Law --UNCITRAL (2004), Legislative Guide on Insolvency Law, Vienna.

von Thadden, E., E. Berglöf and G. Roland (2010), "The Design of Corporate Debt Structure and Bankruptcy", Review of Financial Studies, Vol. 23.

Westmore, B. (2013), "R&D, Patenting and Productivity: The Role of Public Policy", OECD Economics Department Working Paper, No. 1046.

World Bank (2015), "Resolving Insolvency: Measuring the Strength of Insolvency Laws", Doing Business Report, Washington, DC.

Wruck, K. (1990), "Financial Distress, Reorganisation and Organisational Efficiency", Journal of Financial Economics, Vol. 27.

ORGANISATION FOR ECONOMIC CO-OPERATION AND DEVELOPMENT

The OECD is a unique forum where governments work together to address the economic, social and environmental challenges of globalisation. The OECD is also at the forefront of efforts to understand and to help governments respond to new developments and concerns, such as corporate governance, the information economy and the challenges of an ageing population. The Organisation provides a setting where governments can compare policy experiences, seek answers to common problems, identify good practice and work to co-ordinate domestic and international policies.

The OECD member countries are: Australia, Austria, Belgium, Canada, Chile, the Czech Republic, Denmark, Estonia, Finland, France, Germany, Greece, Hungary, Iceland, Ireland, Israel, Italy, Japan, Korea, Latvia, Luxembourg, Mexico, the Netherlands, New Zealand, Norway, Poland, Portugal, the Slovak Republic, Slovenia, Spain, Sweden, Switzerland, Turkey, the United Kingdom and the United States. The European Union takes part in the work of the OECD.

OECD Publishing disseminates widely the results of the Organisation's statistics gathering and research on economic, social and environmental issues, as well as the conventions, guidelines and standards agreed by its members.

OECD PUBLISHING, 2, rue André-Pascal, 75775 PARIS CEDEX 16
(12 2018 01 1 P) ISBN 978-92-64-29195-9 – 2018

www.ingramcontent.com/pod-product-compliance
Lightning Source LLC
LaVergne TN
LVHW081412110826
845149LV00010B/1714

* 9 7 8 9 2 6 4 2 9 1 9 5 9 *